GW00890663

BlackBook List

San Francisco

2006

Restaurants, Bars, Clubs, Hotels

WWW.BLACKBOOKMAG.COM

The BlackBook List is your covert guide to San Francisco's shining culinary stars, dimly lit dive bars and everything in between. Whether you're searching for a strong pour to soothe your nerves, a romantic enclave with that perfect corner table or somewhere to indulge in a night of unprecedented debauchery, these listings offer a variety of select restaurants, bars, clubs and hotels to choose from in every price range.

*Disclaimer: The contents of this manual may be hazardous to your health. Always employ discretion when heading out into the night. Proceed with caution. Good luck.

ISBN # 1932942122 $9.95
© 2005 BlackBook Media Corp.
678 Broadway, 2nd Floor
New York, NY 10012
All rights reserved

This handy manual is an expanded edition of the cult classic Little BlackBook List published
inside of *BlackBook* magazine since 1997, covering nightlife around the globe.

The editorial content, voice, and integrity of the BlackBook List is 100 percent unadulterated. All content & design in this book are the explicit property of BlackBook Media Corp. All possible steps have been taken to ensure that the information in this book is accurate. San Francisco's restaurants and nightspots have the shelf life of your average carton of milk, so some information may have changed. If this is the case, please visit our website at www.blackbookmag.com for accurate listings.

BlackBook List

CREATIVE

SENIOR EDITOR
Irene Ricasio Edwards

ASSOCIATE EDITORS
Andrew Bangs, Fernando Cwilich-Gil

ART DIRECTOR
Tamara Wiesen

DESIGNER
Jillian Blume

CONTRIBUTING WRITERS AND RESEARCHERS
Bryan Abrams, Alison Bing, Hope Bryson, Jason Edwards,
Melissa Goldstein, Tracy Hankins, Rebecca Harper,
Marc Leandro, Hannah Love, Anna Mantzaris, Sue Pierce,
Karen Reardanz, Aron Shafran, Eric Wilinski

PROOFREADER
Daria Brit Shapiro

PRODUCTION DIRECTOR
Amy Steinhauser

SPECIAL THANKS
Pauling, Clifford, J3, Pauli, Yosh and 826 Valencia,
Paul Lawrence, Mary Jane, Hudar, the 6D gals

BLACKBOOK MEDIA CORP.

678 Broadway, 2nd Floor, New York, NY 10012
CEO Eric Gertler
President Ari Horowitz
Publisher Jyl Elias   **GM, BlackBook List** Brian Kantor
Editor in Chief Aaron Hicklin   **Managing Editor** Jess Holl
Art Director Eddie Brannan   **Photography Director** Stephanie Waxlax
Senior Editor Jordan Heller   **Fashion Director** Elizabeth Sulcer
Executive Assistants Candice Naboicheck, Serena D'Arcangelo

To purchase a copy of the *BlackBook List*,
send $9.95 via check or money order to:
BlackBook 678 Broadway 2nd floor
NYC, NY 10012.

Want your restaurant, bar, club, or hotel to be considered for the
BlackBook Lists? Submit your information at www.blackbookmag.com

To purchase a copy of the *BlackBook List* online
or subscibe to *BlackBook* Magazine:

WWW.BLACKBOOKMAG.COM

Table of Contents

How to use

   BlackBook = BlackBook List Editor's Pick
         ☆ = recent opening

Listings are arranged alphabetically by neighborhood. The dollar amount after each listing represents the average cost of a two-course meal and a drink. A plus sign (+) before the number means your bill may be north of that figure. A minus sign (-) means you may have cab money home.

THE DIRECTORY

San Francisco Convention and Visitors Bureau 201 Third St., Ste. 900 (415) 391-2000 Before you tackle the hills, you best learn the ropes.

EMERGENCY & ESSENTIAL DIGITS

Bayview Station (415) 671-2300 If ever in Bayview, memorize this number.
California Pacific Medical Center (415)-600-6000 CPMC for the initiated.
Central Station (415) 315-2400 Not nearly as tough as South Central station.
Mission Station (415) 558-5400 Way hipper than other stations.
Non-Emergency Police Service (415) 553-0123 Loud, obnoxious neighbors.
Poison Control Center 1-800-523-2222 When projectile vomiting gets old.
Police General Services Phone (SF Dispatch) 415-553-8090 Loud, obnoxious armed robbers.
Saint Francis Memorial Hospital (415) 353-6300 Pale green interior really is calming.
San Francisco Fire Department (415) 558-3200 Shiny red engines and Dalmatians.
San Francisco General Hospital (415) 206-8111 All the drama, twice as much blood.
Southern Station (415) 553-1373 Fighting crime with southern accents.
Tenderloin Station (415) 345-7300 Busting johns since '91.
University of California Medical Center (415) 476-1037 Think Scrubs, only uglier.

BUS, CABLE CAR, FERRY, TRAIN & UNDERGROUND INFO

Dial 511 for free traffic and public transport info.
Amtrak (800) 872-7245 Less annoying than bus by far.
AC Transit (buses to Berkeley, Oakland, and other East Bay stops) (510) 839-2882 Getting across the bay without style.
BART (415) 989-2278 Admit it, how they tunneled under the bay baffles you.
Blue and Gold Fleets (to Oakland, Vallejo, and Alcatraz Island) (415) 705-5444 Get toasted on your way to Yoshi's.
Cable Cars (415) 673-MUNI Touristy and cool at the same time.
Caltrain (800) 660-4287 Getting you to San Jose, God knows why?
Golden Gate Ferry (to Sausalito and Larkspur) (415) 455-2000 Water! The GG Bridge! Fog! Woot woot!
Greyhound (800) 231-2222 More annoying than Amtrak by far.
MUNI (city buses) (415) 673-MUNI For fans of stuffy, confined, brutally slow transit situations.

Red and White Fleet (ferries to Angel Island, Muir Woods, Sausalito, and the Wine Country) (800) 229-2784 Kicks the crap out of Blue and Gold fleets.

SamTrans (buses to San Mateo County, including SF International Airport) 800-660-4287 When you just have to get to San Mateo.

CAR SERVICE, SHUTTLE & TAXI

American Airporter Shuttle (415) 546-6689 For the patriots among us.

Bay Shuttle (415) 564-3400 Kinda like Ocean Shuttle, just smaller.

De Soto Cab (415) 970-1300 Snobby but efficient.

Luxor Cab (415) 282-4141 Named after city in Central Egypt, for obvious reasons.

Quicksilver Town Car (800) 486-9622 Bit of an overstatement, but the A/C sure feels nice.

Yellow Cab (415) 626-2345 More cowardly than other cabs.

LIBRARY

San Francisco Public Library (Main Branch) 100 Larkin St. (Grove St.) (415) 557-4400 Giving other branches a size complex.

MUSEUMS

Asian Art Museum 200 Larkin St. (McAllister & Grove Sts.) (415) 581-3500 More than 14,000 works from the collection of Avery Brundage, a rich guy with an Asian fetish.

Cable Car Museum 1201 Mason St. (Washington St.) (415) 474-1887 Hey, they're faster than MUNI.

California Academy of Sciences 875 Howard St. (4th & 5th Sts.) (415) 321-8000 Blinding you with science, daily penguin feeding a plus.

Cartoon Art Museum 655 Mission St. (3rd & New Montgomery Sts.) (415) 227-8666 Best viewed in pajamas while eating Cap'n Crunch.

De Young Museum 50 Tea Garden Dr. (415) 750-3600 Wicked-stepmother socialite guilt-tripped her rich friends into giving up the loot for this one.

Exploratorium 3601 Lyon St. (Richardson & Marina Blvds.) (415) 563-7337 Asian brides posing for cheesy photo op.

Legion of Honor 34th Ave. (Clement St.) (415) 863-3330 Lives up to its dramatic title.

Musée Mécanique Pier 45 (Embarcadero Blvd. & Taylor St.) (415) 346-2000 Couple hundred vintage coin-operated machines, fortune tellers, music boxes, creepy clowns. Go sober.

Museum of Modern Art 151 3rd St. (Mission & Howard Sts.) (415) 357-4000 Kickass art, artsy parties.

Ripley's Believe it or Not 175 Jefferson St. (Mason & Taylor Sts.) (415) 771-6188 Go here… or Not.

San Francisco Museum of Craft & Folk Art Fort Mason Center, Building A (415) 775-0990 Crafty, folksy, the whole nine.

Tattoo Art Museum 841 Columbus Ave. (Lombard St.) (415) 775-4991 Couple notches up from anything you're sporting.

The Wax Museum at Fisherman's Wharf 145 Jefferson St. (Mason & Taylor Sts.) (415) 885-4834 The chamber of horrors is wax gone bad.

STADIUMS & CONCERT VENUES

Bill Graham Civic Auditorium 99 Grove St. (Larkin St.) (415) 974-4000 Named after the guy who revolutionized concertgoing by stuffing dangerous amounts of people into any venue he could. Genius.

Bottom of the Hill 1233 17th St. (Missouri St.) (415) 621-4455 Sunday BBQs, music galore.

The Fillmore 1805 Geary Blvd. (Fillmore St.) (415) 346-6000 The memorabilia on the walls alone warrants a visit.

Great American Music Hall 859 O'Farrell St. (Polk St.) (415) 885-0750 Rocking out, bordello-style.

Greek Theatre Gayley Rd., Berkeley (415) 421-8497 A touch of ancient Greece in hippie-infested Berkeley. Sick venue, with or without the hash brownies.

Monster Park Candlestick Point (Jamestown Ave.) (415) 656-4900 Joe Montana has left the building.

Network Associates Coliseum 7000 Coliseum Way, Oakland (510) 569-2121 Bust out your Darth Vader mask with the rest of Raider Nation.

Paramount Theatre 2025 Broadway, Oakland (20th & 21st Sts.) Soul divas and African-American mamas putting on the Ritz.

SBC Park 24 Willie Mays Plaza (3rd St.) (415) 972-2000 Sip Merlot and eat Ben & Jerry's while watching Barry go yard.

Shoreline Amphitheatre One Amphitheatre Parkway, Mountain View (650) 967-3000 Alas, it's nowhere near the ocean

THEATER & PERFORMING ARTS

Actor's Theatre of San Francisco 533 Sutter St. (Powell & Mason Sts.) (415) 296-9179 Debuting the work of Mamets and Bogosians.

American Conservatory Theater 415 Geary St. (Mason & Taylor Sts.) (415) 729-2ACT SF's flagship theater. Expensive seats and bad parking part of the charm.

Buriel Clay Theatre 762 Fulton St. (Webster St.) (415) 292-1850 Comic cabaret ensembles that just scream San Francisco.

City Arts & Lectures Herbst Theatre, 401 Van Ness Ave. (McAllister St.) (415) 392-4400 If you just can't get enough of Dave Eggers.

EXIT Theatre 156 Eddy St. (Mason & Taylor Sts.) (415) 931-1094 Unstuffy, not staid, it's a boho delight.

Glide Memorial 330 Ellis St. (Taylor St. & Jones St.) (415) 674-6000 Get your God on, complete with trannies and the homeless—Tenderloin-style!

Magic Theatre Fort Mason Center, Building D (415) 441-8822 Free parking, two theatres, 30 years of service. We bow to you, Magic.

San Francisco Ballet War Memorial Opera House, 301 Van Ness Ave. (Grove St.) (415) 861-5600 Great chick magnet.

San Francisco Opera War Memorial Opera House, 301 Van Ness Ave. (Grove St.) (415) 864-3330 Hi, we're loaded.

San Francisco Symphony Davies Symphony Hall, 201 Van Ness Ave. (Grove St.) (415) 864-6000 Getting all Stradivarius on your ass.

Yerba Buena Center for the Arts 700 Howard St. (3rd St.) (415) 978-2787 Pickup spot of choice for intellectuals.

PARKS, GARDENS & BEACHES

Alcatraz Island Ferry departs from Pier 41 (415) 705-5444 Don't do the crime if you can't do the time.

Baker Beach West of the GG Bridge, in the Presidio. Nice view of San Francisco's Golden Arches.

China Beach Base of Seacliff, Golden Gate Park. Small, sheltered, sandy beach for low-key lounging or getting rid of evidence.

Crissy Field Along Marina Blvd. Formerly a military airstrip, now a 100-acre waterfront park perfect for the kids!

Golden Gate Park Corner of Stanyan & Fulton Sts. (415) 561-4700 1,017 acres of pure nature bliss. Arboretums, gardens, lakes, playgrounds, golf course, conservatory of flowers, soccer fields, tea garden, bison, bowling greens, people smoking greens, etc.

Japanese Tea Garden Inside Golden Gate Park (415) 668-0909 Small Japanese oasis complete with loud tourists from Iowa.

Ocean Beach The entire west side of SF. Windy to the point of hilarity, but very long, very strong, at times it gets the friction on.

Rodeo Beach Marin County. An alarmingly small amount of actual rodeo takes place here, but if it did there'd be naked cowboys.

Stinson Beach Marin County. Nearly a mile of pristine beach, sharks in the water an added bonus.

AIRPORTS

Oakland International Airport 1 Airport Dr. Fly into Oaktown and prove you've got soul.

San Francisco International Airport Off Highway 101, McDonnell Rd. Because everyone's comfortable with fog-draped runways.

San Jose Airport 1661 Airport Blvd. People seem happier departing San Jose for some reason. Weird.

"The coldest winter I ever saw was the summer I spent in San Francisco." —Mark Twain

Top 5 Best Developments in SF Nightlife
(Keeping the dream alive)

1. **Late-Night Coalition**
   Fighting for your right to party till 4 a.m.
2. **Underground loft parties**
   Fire code violation, but fun as hell
3. **Dot-com bomb shelter**
   Artists in, yuppies out
4. **Hotter chicks**
   Imported from NY or LA for your viewing pleasure
5. **Class system in the mix**
   Danielle Steel next to RZA…now we're talking

TOP 5 Most Illicit Bathrooms
(For powdering your nose or freaking on the sink)

1. **Frisson**
   Unisex stalls aplenty
2. **Zuni Cafe**
   Homage to the late great '80s
3. **Hotel Biron**
   Dark alleyway action
4. **The Stud**
   Gay dive extraordinaire
5. **Any Nob Hill hotel**
   Private stalls and attendants with real towels!

TOP 5 Places to Make an Ass out of Yourself
(But really, the possibilities are endless)

1. **The Mint**
   Karaoke in the Castro, say no more
2. **MatrixFillmore**
   Marina bimbos at their sleaziest
3. **City Tavern**
   Big cheap beers lead to obstreperous conversation
4. **AsiaSF**
   Gender benders bringing out the best
5. **Blondies**
   Sidewalk seats make for serious sketch comedy

TOP 5 Costliest Buzz

(Aside from the Peruvian stuff, that is)

1. **Frisson**
   Euro trash don't come cheap
2. **Gold Club**
   View's pretty good, too
3. **Otis**
   Membership has its privileges…doesn't it?
4. **Fifth Floor Lounge on 5**
   1,400 wines and counting
5. **Four Seasons Bar**
   Honchos of an Asian persuasion

TOP 5 Most Orgasmic Food Experiences

(Heavy breathing a plus)

1. **Tsar Nicoulai**
   Truffle oil, eggs and caviar
2. **Zuni Café**
   Roast chicken for two
3. **Canteen**
   Helluva cassoulet
4. **Gary Danko**
   Cheese cart action
5. **El Farolito**
   Quesadilla pechuga with carne asada

TOP 5 Dance Floors for Tearing it Up

(With or without the party favors)

1. **The EndUp**
   Freakin' since 1973
2. **Rx Gallery**
   Pill popping required
3. **Nickie's BBQ**
   Rolling with the homies
4. **Arrow Bar**
   '80s revival to the max
5. **The Stud**
   Mostly dudes, obviously, but fag hags dance in peace

TOP 5 Places to Spot SF "Celebs"

(Beggars can't be choosers)

1. **Chanel store party**
   Selma Blair and Stephan Jenkins
2. **Tosca**
   Coppola famiglia in the back room
3. **Gold's Gym SoMa**
   Benjamin Bratt in a sweaty knit cap
4. **Plumpjack Café**
   No denying our mayor's a hottie
5. **SF Ballet opening**
   Paris Hilton in a tutu

TOP 5 Places to Pretend You're a Baller

(Equal-opportunity posin')

1. **The Big Four**
   Dude, they built the railroad
2. **Gary Danko**
   Tour the wine cellar if you're lucky
3. **Top of the Mark**
   Blow your wad 19 floors aboveground
4. **Otis**
   I'm a member, dammit
5. **Mitchell Brothers**
   Bigger bag of tricks

TOP 5 Spots to Score with a Slutty Chick

(But you didn't hear it from us)

1. **MatrixFillmore**
   Young, dumb, full of c-m
2. **Tunnel Top**
   Working-class gals with hearts of gold
3. **Harry Denton's Starlight Room**
   Collagenized cougars
4. **Red Devil Lounge**
   Rocker 'hos
5. **Redwood Room**
   Gold diggers galore

TOP 5 Places to Indulge Your Inner Cheeseball

(We wear our sunglasses at night)

1. **suite one8one**
   Bottle service on the center bed
2. **Ruby Skye**
   Cigars on a Saturday night
3. **Harry Denton's Rouge**
   Studmasters in tricked-out Civics
4. **Bubble Lounge**
   First you gotta learn how to spell Cristal
5. **Tonga Room**
   Leftover pot stickers and floating cover band

TOP 5 Hottest Chefs

(These folks are on fire)

1. **Dennis Leary, Canteen**
   In a weird strawberry-blond intense kinda way
2. **Gerald Hirigoyen, Piperade**
   Gerard Depardieu with a toque
3. **Laurent Manrique, Aqua**
   Silky smooth Frenchie, just like his foie
4. **Melissa Perello, Fifth Floor**
   Corn-fed cutie patootie
5. **Ola Fendert, Oola**
   Viking at the stove

TOP 5 Spots to Get Sloshed Outdoors

(Hang it all out for the world to see)

1. **Bambuddha Lounge**
   But only before 11 p.m.
2. **Zeitgeist**
   Hit up the tamale lady
3. **Pier 23**
   Sports bar with a view
4. **Lucky 13**
   Rockers get their nicotine fix
5. **El Rio**
   Flygirl action on the patio

UNION SQUARE &
FINANCIAL DISTRICT (map p.114)

Bottle-blond heiresses emerge from Gucci, Bottega, and Vuitton. Out-of-towners converge on Neiman's and Saks in chattering droves. Now there's an H&M and a Bloomingdale's—the shopping nirvana is complete! Welcome to **Union Square**, SF's own miniature Madison Avenue. **Got some cash burning a hole in your pocket? Come on down!** As for hotels, we'll start with our fat-cat favorite, the Four Seasons, backlit with the glow of adulterous flirtation amid so much burnished wealth. (Note to desperate housewives looking for a little extra attention: The personal trainers at the Sports Club/LA are well up for it.) Belden Lane is a fun Euro pickup scene best avoided on Bastille Day, when mobs storm the premises like it's 1789. Over in the **Financial** side of things, pinstriped young whippersnappers shriek into their phones with elation or despair. All the action takes place in the early hours, and it's a ghost town by 8 pm. Down on the water-front is the Ferry Building, one of SF's crown jewels, with its orgasmatron spread of gourmet delicacies and organic produce; think food market gone to heaven, with prices to match. We kinda liked the humbler version, but we're all for farmers getting their due. You'll find us getting raucous with the laddies over fish n' chips at the **Irish Bank** before moving on to sidecars served up by Adam at **Tadich Grill**. For dessert: a slice of naughty behavior à la mode at **Globe**.

RESTAURANTS Union Square & Financial District

Armani Café 1 Grant Ave. (O'Farrell St.) (415) 677-9010. Italiano. From Giorgio with love. Shopping and lunch in one fell swoop. Will it be the mock turtleneck or the frisee salad? Tables on the sidewalk to linger in the sun. Buttoned-up Macy's execs, young magazine chicks in Costume National. Antipasto plate is the way to go. $25

Asia de Cuba 495 Geary St. (Jones & Taylor Sts.) (415) 929-2300 Upscale Chino-Latino. Twenty-five-foot ceilings, plush velvet drapery, and mirrored communal table shaped like a cross make this Philippe Starck design the Three Tenors of high theater. Calamari salad with hearts of palm and banana? Tuna tartare with black currants and coconut? Against all logic, it works. Hottest servers in town. +$50

Boulevard 1 Mission St. (Steuart St.) (415) 543-6084 French/New American. Decadent Belle Epoque meets inspired, impeccable cuisine. Wrought-iron lamps dangle gracefully from brick ceilings, waiters sail smoothly through a sea of bejeweled ladies, and fat-cat men grin like Cheshire at the sight of wood oven–roasted fish and meats. Wanting for nothing, wishing you had it more often. All-around pleasure. $65

Cafe Claude 7 Claude Lane (Grant Ave. & Kearny St./Sutter & Bush Sts.) (415) 392-3515 French. Romantic, in a let's-get-it-on-in-this-alley kind of way. Sassy bartender, sexy candlelight, simply French food. Wednesday is ladies' night, with $3 cocktails and entrees at girl-friendly discount. Intimate Euro feel attracts international crowd in the mood for love, or at least sharing the fondue for two. $35

Colibrí Mexican Bistro 438 Geary St. (Mason & Taylor Sts.) (415) 440-2737 Mexican. Three Amigos bistro welcomes businessmen on holiday and margarita-slurping theater crowd. You think you know tequila? Prove it. Tableside-mashed guacamole with bottomless supply of steamed tortillas paired with pricy nouveaux Latino cocktails. Who says mojitos aren't Mexican? This crowd's not complaining. $30 ☆

Fifth Floor 12 4th St. (Market St.) (415) 348-1555 Contemporary French. How do you say decadence? Could it be the rabbit with apple and salsify? Truffles and scallops? Chef Melissa Perello has the answer. Zebra-striped rug, so you know you're in for a good time. Culinary showstopper, with prices to prove it. +$60

First Crush 101 Cyril Magnin St. (Ellis St.) (415) 982-7874 Progressive American. Understated business for lunch, dazed tourists and Armani Exchange–attired city slickers livin' large by night. Happy hour catering to newbie wine connoisseurs. Labyrinthian watering hole with live jazz and California-only wine list. $45

Frisson 244 Jackson St. (Sansome St.) (415) 956-3004 New American. Hey New York, we can stay up late too. Horny young attorneys and visiting "industry" folk mingling with frisky fillies over cocktails with sprigs. Glowing overhead dome, mid-century swivel chairs, curvaceous banquettes, private rooms, dollhouse-sized portions, three-girls-in-one-bathroom-stall all very Less Than Zero. Sci-fi frothy carrot soup—yes, frothy, like your cappuccino. +$50 ☆

Globe 290 Pacific Ave. (Battery & Front Sts.) (415) 391-4132 New American. Little piece of SoHo in Jackson Square. Late-night Cinderella catering to fine-dining needs: freshly shucked oysters, grilled lamb T-bone, huge pork chop, gnocchi with oxtail ragout, all till 1 a.m. Off-duty chefs arrive after hanging up toques for the evening. Tight quarters make for biblical cacophony, but get into it, speak up, have fun. $35

Hog Island Oyster Co. 1 Ferry Building. (Embarcadero Blvd. & Market St.) (415) 391-7177 Oyster bar. Only one thing on your mind: ocean. Businessmen, epicures, ferry-riding tourists elbow-to-elbow at granite-topped bar in Ferry Building food mall. Robust young men shuck away furiously in front of you, while behind them lies the bay and the wild blue yonder. Oysters harvested an hour away and delivered daily, still glistening with briny sea. Nice wine list. $35

Jeanty at Jack's 615 Sacramento (Kearny & Montgomery Sts.) (415) 693-0941 French. Landmark building housing oldest restaurant in San Francisco. Originally opened in 1864 , favorite eatery for Hitchcock back in the day. Third-floor private dining rooms rumored to be for other pleasures. Fourth floor topped with enormous vaulted skylight, casting a glow on Hermès-clad ladies and gentlemen in dapper bow ties. Astonishing architectural space brimming with history and charm. $40

Kokkari 200 Jackson St. (Front St.) (415) 981-0983 Greek. Gorgeous room, rustic and elegant, with burning hearths and big floral arrangements. Friendly, slightly leering waiters add authentic Mediterranean flavor. Get the crisp fried smelt, grilled octopus, and creamy salt cod brandade. Discreet and moneyed clientele, subtle upper-crust pickup scene at the bar. +40

Le Central 453 Bush St. (Grant Ave. & Kearny St.) (415) 391-2233 French. SF institution for more than 30 years, favored meeting spot for city's colorful elite. Regulars include late great journalist Herb Caen and da ex-mayor himself, Willie Brown. Cassoulet simmering continuously from the mother sauce for nearly 11,000 days. Personal-size ice bucket keeps overflow of martini chilled just so. History like only an insider would see it. $30

Lefty O'Douls 333 Geary St. (Powell & Mason Sts.) (415) 982-8900 Hofbrau buffet. Opened in 1958 by eccentric SF baseball personality. Memorabilia-packed hole in one for sports fanatics and fans of barbarian-style grub. Gorge on slabs of prime rib or, on the lighter side, a leg of turkey. Frat guys and random tourist families hunkering down till midnight to live jazz piano. $20

MarketBar 1 Ferry Building (Embarcadero & Market St.) (415) 434-1100 California brasserie. Season's freshest bounty, served up amid Saturday farmers' market, under a festive umbrella, or on the sidewalk by the bay. Ingredients so beautiful they could be porn. Lunch crowd brimming with office workers soaking up precious rays of sun. Come happy hour, handsome dark wood bar packs 'em in for lubricating elixirs. $36

Masa's Restaurant 648 Bush St. (Powell St.) (415) 989-7154 French. Chicer alternative to chintz at the Ritz. Local haute cuisine journey for those out of luck at French Laundry. Dining room is unexpectedly designer, with deep chocolate walls, to-the-floor Frette, some hammered sculpture action, red lanterns, and modern toile all showcasing 4-, 6-, or 9-course feasts. No surprises, no regrets. Carts abound. Guys: Wear your Brioni jacket. $100

Millennium 580 Geary St. (Jones & Taylor Sts.) (415) 345-3900 Vegan. Upscale oasis for those who eschew chewing on animals and their byproducts. Creative vegan gourmet without hint of scruffy hippie trappings. Pecan crusted portabella and creamy roasted garlic polenta is actually delicious! Organic cocktails, house-infused vodkas at long, stately bar. Bring meat-loving Midwesterners and show them how good it can get. $37

New Delhi 160 Ellis St. (Cyril Magnin St.) (415) 397-8470 Northern Indian. Not exactly Jewel in the Crown, but for 17 years a mainstay of SF's Indian population. Regal space with floor-to-ceiling columns and posters of maharajahs. Full bar stays open long after the kitchen, so restaurant workers ending their shifts at neighboring joints can wind down over a cocktail or two to the penetrating aroma of curry. $30

Ozumo 161 Steuart St. (Mission St.) (415) 882-1333 Japanese. At 5 pm sharp begins the charge. Infantry unit of downtown workers floods front bar with blue dress shirts, pinstripe suits, and hosiery. Back room like Tokyo in Vegas on Xanax washed down with flight of unfiltered sake. Business diners and sexy couples feeding on spendy sashimi and Kobe-style morsels from robata. +$47

Plouf 40 Belden Place (Kearny & Montgomery Sts./Pine & Bush Sts.) (415) 986-6491 French Seafood. Like Gallic theme park, where flirty-birdy waiters in nautical striped shirts make eyes at the ladies and bestow slobbery kisses. No matter, this dark and sexy eatery can't help but seduce. Sit in the alley and get mussels one of seven different ways. Heavy petting a plus. $36

Restaurant Michael Mina 335 Powell St. (Geary St.) (415) 397-9222 Contemporary American. We brake for socialites. Wedding-reception décor in lighter shade of pale to match clientele. Only heathens skip straight to the entree. Discuss family business with Mummy over Tom Collins and Choose-Your-Own-Adventure three-course menu. Billed as next big thing, with bill to match. $60 ☆

The Rotunda Restaurant at Neiman Marcus 150 Stockton St. (Geary St.) (415) 362-4777 Contemporary American. Central Casting doing ladies who lunch. Atop venerable institution of needless markups, below impressive stained-glass rotunda built in 1909. Daily tea service stars crustless sandwiches and dainty pastries, with scene-stealing appearance by righteous puffed-up popovers with strawberry jam. +$25

The Slanted Door 1 Ferry Bldg. (Embarcadero Blvd. & Market St.) (415) 861-8329 Vietnamese-California fusion. Recently opened new location of gourmet favorite. Huge and bustling room aswarm with fashionable eaters. Food as sparklingly fresh and invigorating as the ocean view. Noisy as a lunchroom cafeteria, but sounds are happy ones. Eclectic crowd feasting on cellophane noodles with crab, claypot catfish, spicy squid. Everything Charles Phan touches turns to gastronomic gold. Yes please, and then some. +$37 **BlackBook**

Tadich Grill 240 California St. (Battery & Front Sts.) (415) 391-1849 Seafood. Opened during Gold Rush as tent-covered coffee stand by three Croatian immigrants. Old-world feel kept alive by enormous wraparound bar, private wood-paneled booths, and all-male waitstaff in starchy white aprons. Menu is all about the ocean, with classics like shrimp louie and bursting cioppino. And yes, they will bring you a bib. Place to impress a business lunch, or to dazzle out-of-towners. $37

Tartare 550 Washington St. (Montgomery and Sansome Sts.) (415) 434-3100 Contemporary American. Raw bar stages coup d'état in kitchen. Beef tartare, ahi tuna tartare, ostrich tartare, medium well need not apply. Big-shot chef George Morrone makes undercooked the new cooked. Sunset-glow lighting, Armani suits negotiating Indonesian pickled vegetables while negotiating deals. I'll get this one—it's on the company. $60 ★

Taylor's Automatic Refresher 1 Ferry Building (Embarcadero Blvd. & Market St.) (866) 328-3663 Hamburgers. That most American of meals taken to foodie heights. Only organic, never-frozen beef, locally farmed produce, impressive California wine list. Have your bacon double cheeseburger and support sustainable agriculture at the same time. Top off your karma with a thick 'n' rich milkshake, made with local Double Rainbow ice cream. $12

Town Hall 342 Howard St. (Fremont & Beale Sts.) (415) 908-3900 New American. Recently conceived brainchild of seasoned SF restaurateurs gives dining scene a much-needed shot in the arm. Big windows, rich wooden tables, exposed brick walls setting off inspired twists on rootsy classics. Start with the romaine lettuce salad with cornmeal-fried oysters, and let the freefall begin. Sit communal-style and rub designer bags with the hungry downtown set. +$43

Tsar Nicoulai Caviar Café 1 Ferry Building (Embarcadero Blvd. & Market St.) (415) 288-8630 Caviar Bar. You know those days when you really want to treat yourself? Indulge in the most luxurious snacking this planet can offer. Wide range of caviar presented with careful detail, like truffled scrambled egg served in its shell, or sturgeon sashimi in a clear glass cone submerged in a water-filled bowl swimming with live fish. and delicious. $35 **BlackBook**

Yank Sing Restaurant 101 Spear St. (Mission & Howard Sts.) (415) 957-9300 Dim sum. Get your dumpling on in high style at this impressively clean, consistently delectable dim sum dreamland. Sinfully rich egg custards, BBQ pork buns, stuffed lotus leaves, even vegetarian treats like snow pea shoot dumplings and mango pudding. Not the cheapest, but one of the best. +$27

NIGHTLIFE Union Square & Financial District

Azul 1 Tillman Place (Post & Sutter Sts.) (415) 362-9750 Shake off your workaday blues in the cool blue vibe of a dark and velvety den. Happy hour draws working stiffs, but as the night melts on, so does the attitude. Yowza! Collars loosen, attitudes chill, and soon everyone's swaying to live Latin jazz. All juices are fresh-squeezed, so try the sour pineapple martini.

Cortez 550 Geary St. (Taylor & Jones Sts.) (415) 292-6360 Modern art on the mind at the Hotel Adagio lounge. Behind the bar = homage to Mondrian. Sculptural mobile lamps = shout-out to Calder, with bit of the Jetsons thrown in for fun. Ladies in sequined tops + bespectacled gents in town for a dreary conference = boozy good time, with morning-after regrets.

Four Seasons Hotel Bar 757 Market St. (3rd & 4th Sts.) (415) 633-3737 Sure, the drinks are pricey, but you enjoy them in high style. And in hand-blown glasses, yet. Elite world travelers mingling discreetly with sophisticated after-work boozers quietly getting lit on labor-intensive cocktails as nightly live piano drifts through the air. Colorful array of endless bar snacks offsets dent in your wallet, somewhat. **BlackBook**

Gold Dust Lounge 247 Powell St. (Geary & O'Farrell Sts.) (415) 397-1695 Shucks, it's Kitty and the crew from Gunsmoke. Saloon-esque watering hole with gold-brocade wallpaper, red velvet booths, mural of cavorting cherubs on the ceiling. Trapdoor once housed a pole for topless dancers to slide into the laps of happy drinkers during the '50s, when Bing Crosby owned the joint. Crowd is half tourists, half bartenders, 100 percent hard drinkers.

Harry Denton's Starlight Room 450 Powell St (Post & Sutter Sts.) (415) 395-8595 The setting: crushed-velvet booths on the 21st floor of the Sir Francis Drake Hotel. The crowd: Botoxed bleached blonds wearing leftover prom dresses and escorted by black-tie bucks. The conclusion: Harry is the Hefner of SF nightlife. Portraits of stars in cheap gold frames, stars in your drink lovingly served by a playmate, stars all around you as you gaze out the window.

House of Shields 39 New Montgomery St. (Market & Mission Sts.) (415) 975-8651 Think Baby Face Nelson caressing his platinum-haired moll with the butt of his machine gun. Established in 1908, only watering hole around for years, and a gentleman's-only club till 1972. Prohibition-era speakeasy accessed by secret tunnel from Palace Hotel across the street. Kinda cool since it reinvented itself as a late-night hang with eclectic little parties ranging from hip-hop to house to jazz.

Irish Bank 10 Mark Lane (Grant Ave. & Kearny St.) (415) 788-7152 Now here's a place to get rip-roaring drunk and feel like you're following tradition at the same time. Country-schoolroom look plastered with black-and-white photos of famous Irish drinkers of yore. Cozy little area in back with lantern lamps, alleyway to handle spillage outside. Don't mind the hordes of ruddy frat boys—we can all have fun if we just keep on drinking. **BlackBook**

Johnny Foley's Irish House 243 O'Farrell St. (Cyril Magnin St.) (415) 954-0777 Sweatshirts and stonewashed jeans aside, there's good times to be had at this true drinkers' bar. A tall tale or two to raucous old-time rock 'n' roll will have you in the gutter singing Irish rebel songs before the night is through. You're in good company: Portraits of Oscar Wilde, James Joyce, and Johnny Foley himself (who?) adorn the walls.

London Wine Bar 415 Sansome St. (Sacramento & Clay St.) (415) 788-4811 Unassuming pub-like spot calling itself "America's oldest wine bar." Wanna Philly cheese steak or sausage platter to accompany weekly samples of Zinfandel? Owner/bartender is down-to-earth Deadhead with waist-length ponytail who wants to make wine fun. Downtown drinkers, zero attitude.

The Old Ship Saloon 298 Pacific St. (Battery St.) (415) 788-2222 Heaps o' history seeping from corner of old Barbary Coast. Sailor spirit still alive and well. Ask bartender to show you authentic "Shanghai stick" found in the walls, used to clobber men unconscious and abduct them into a life on the high seas. Raunchy and historical at the same time.

Otis 25 Maiden Ln. (Grant Ave. & Kearny St.) Make up your minds now: Private club or not? Soho House or Studio 54? Boys get A for exclusivity effort, but velvet rope more gesture than reality. Teeny two-tiered space with peacock painting, mirrored snakeskin bar, crocodile-print wallpaper, flashy chandelier. Design often sexier than standard-issue socialite crowd. Plebeians take heart: If you really must, it's open entry before 8 pm (?!). ★

Redwood Room 495 Geary St. (Jones & Taylor Sts.) (415) 929-2372 Once your eyes adjust to the near-darkness, it's a people-watching paradise. Ladies doing it up with tube tops and stilettos, fellas getting swanky with pinstripes and the occasional gold chain. With gorgeous deco lamps and floor-to-ceiling redwood walls, the place was a drinking destination even before Schrager pushed the style envelope. Forever teetering on the edge of good taste, but so pretty you always forgive it.

Voda 56 Belden Pl. (Bush St., Kearny & Montgomery Sts.) (415) 677-9242 You're in a Spike Jonze commercial, starring Chloë Sevigny and backlit by Dan Flavin. Voda is Russian for water, but don't go ordering any of that shit from the all-female bartenders rocking sexy Puma sweats. Roc-A-Fella parties here, and Jay-Z's label is one of 65 vodkas on hand.

White Horse Tavern 635 Sutter St. (Mason & Taylor Sts.) (415) 673-9900 In the center of theater district, quaint English-style pub with good whiskey and thespians unwinding after hitting the boards. Antique maps of Britannia, faux wood beams, and rustic furniture round out Ye Olde English feel. Shotguns and fox-hunting memorabilia push it over the edge. Relax, you're safe from the werewolves prowling the moor.

"I'm heading for that golden gate hoping I won't be to late, to find the one that I still love."

—Chris Isaak

TENDERLOIN & DOWNTOWN (map p. 115)

So, rough and tumble is how you like it? Then this is the neighborhood for you. And for those who think SF is all polar fleece and pastel-colored Victorians, you're in for a surprise. **The grit is palpable here in the 'Loin**, but with a name like that don't say you weren't warned. To the novice it can come off as some 21st-century version of the apocalypse—shirtless junkies with flailing limbs, hard-edged working girls with hiked-up skirts—but trust us, go with it, this is an area on the move. The rewards for those who dare: tasty dives, exotic Asian markets, irresistible tandoor joints, plus undeniable cred. Also the Phoenix Hotel, a longtime rocker hangout that's good enough, sometimes, for the likes of Sofia Coppola. Improbably, there's quite a bit of nightlife around, from amateur pool tourneys at **Café Royale** to messy bachelorette parties at **Bambuddha**. Straight guys get lit and flirt with the busty Malaysian ladyboys on Polk, and to get inside a club you may have to step over someone with a needle in their arm. **For a startling model of urban recovery, see the TenderNob (Downtown), which straddles the tightrope between the 'Loin and Nob Hill—two neighborhoods so diverse you'd think they were on other planets.** It's too much for the tourists, but you said you liked it rough, didn't you? Join us in line for killer banh mi at **Saigon Sandwich Shop**, having a hoot with C. Bobby at the **Owl Tree**, cooling our heels at the counter at **Canteen**, and then picking up our meds yet again at the **Rx Gallery**.

RESTAURANTS Tenderloin & Downtown

Anzu 222 Mason St. (O'Farrell & Ellis Sts.) (415) 394-1111 Japanese Steakhouse/Sushi. Pretty good porterhouse, but only if you can't score a seat at the bar where your eyes can avert the banquet-room like atmosphere. Nod to the Japanese businessmen and watch master chef Katsuhito Takahashi work his magic on creatures from the deep. Don't even try to order, just put yourself in his hands. +$40

Bambuddha Lounge 601 Eddy St. (Larkin St.) (415) 885-5088 Southeast Asian. Flavor of the month with unexpected staying power. Meet me in the cabana, my little Asian flower, where I can feed you sensuously with my chopsticks. Will it be Isaan chicken or Malaysian lamb Rendang? Oh, you naughty little monkey! Let me lure you to the poolside pavilion to complete the seduction. $28

Borobudur 700 Post St. (Leavenworth St.) (415) 775-1512 Indonesian. What it lacks in ambiance, it makes up for in homestyle platters that pack in tables of

Indonesian families. You want the coconut milk-braised barbecue chicken and string beans in earthy shrimp paste. Then you mop it all up with flaky roti prata. $15

Café do Brasil 1106 Market St. (Jones St.) (415) 626-6432 Brazilian. All-you-can-eat churrasco rodizio (Brazilian barbecue) Thursday through Sunday. As for the salad bar, you're better off at Sizzler. The odd live samba extravaganza with show-girls, sequins, feathers, the works, ay yay yay! Just steer clear of the hustlers on Market Street. $25

Canteen 817 Sutter St. (Jones St.) (415) 928-8870 Californian-French. Tall chef in tiny space. Think David and Goliath: cubbyhole-sized spot (20 seats max) with cof-fee-shop vibe, petite menu and mini wine list, but chef Dennis Leary casting shad-ow of greatness. Crispy pork belly battles veal pot pie. Settle in at Granny Smith–colored counter with the paper, since big, big treat equals long, long wait. Word is out on sleeper success. $42 ★ **BlackBook**

Chai Yo 1331 Polk St. (Bush St.) (415) 771-2562 Thai. Cute cartoon girl on sign keeps second-rate rockers stopping in on their way to the Hemlock for one-plate dinners of green papaya salad, barbecue chicken, and sticky rice. Next-door sweets shop with tapioca tea, ice cream, treats wrapped in banana leaves, even Thai videos (no, not the kinky kind). $15

Chutney 511 Jones St. (O'Farrell St.) (415) 931-5541 Indian. Of all the Indian-Pakistani dives in the Tandoor-loin, Chutney is the cleanest. Are those sconces on the walls? Handsome Indian boy takes your order, gives you a number, and you grab your own water and chai. Huge puffed-up naan, all the right curries, plus exot-ic specials like goat in fiery tomato sauce. Young Asian families chow down next to groups of white-bread types who've brought their own Cab. $15

Dottie's True Blue Cafe 522 Jones St. (O'Farrell St.) (415) 885-2767 American diner. We won't lie to you, the weekend wait is hell—especially after a night of too many margaritas—but the supersized homestyle breakfasts are for reals. Pesto, andouille, and goat-cheese omelet with a slice of buttermilk dill bread will set you straight. Cleanse your liver and then cleanse your soul at Glide Memorial. $10

Fleur de Lys 777 Sutter St. (Jones St.) (415) 673-7779 Haute French. Voilà, romance! Brought to you by owner-chef Hubert Keller. Tented dining area with gar-gantuan floral centerpiece, but if you're a real high-roller, you'll be supping in one of the private rooms. Vegetarian tasting menu is splendid, so is foie gras in brioche "burger." Stiff crowd, stiffer prices. Ouch. +$50 ★

La'zeez 25 Mason St. (Turk St.) (415) 771-5503 Asian Fusion. Menu hits up most of Asia, plus fruity cocktails and bar bites—get the Asian wings with your Asian Lady. Down-and-out neighborhood, but things are a little calmer here for the sake of Lion King fans. Hip-hop on Fridays keeps the fusion thing going. $25

Le Colonial 20 Cosmo Pl. (Sutter & Post Sts., Taylor & Jones Sts.) (415) 931-3600 Vietnamese. Lazy ceiling fans, bamboo birdcages, palms waving softly in the breeze… sigh. Sexy Indochine atmosphere marred by Banana Republic–clad singles sucking down after-work cocktails. Skip the main menu and order spring rolls and crab cakes from the lounge. Save room for the chocolate and peanut butter spring rolls, oh mama they be good. $45

Mela 417 O'Farrell St. (Taylor St.) (415) 447-4041 Indian. Setting worthy of Indiana Jones, with street scene right out of Calcutta. Gurgling fountain, pressed tin ceilings and framed dolls, low tables and murals of Indian palaces. Soundtrack culled from the latest Bollywood premiere (note to DJ: bhangra and trance not always winning dinner combination). Some curries can be nuclear hot. $10

Naan 'N' Curry 478 O'Farrell St. (Jones St.) (415) 775-1349 Indian. Wade your way through the street theatrics and brace yourself for the tandoor blast. Hot damn! Crispy naan brushed with ghee, tandoor lamb chops—five of them—fiery enough to keep you heading back to the cooler. Best value of all the Indian spots around. $10

Osha Thai Noodle Café 696 Geary Blvd. (Leavenworth St.) (415) 673-2368 Thai. Perfect late-night fix in the Tenderloin, food-wise, at least. Younger sister on Valencia might be cuter, but this one set the mold. Gamine waitresses bring hot plates of noodles with duck and Chinese broccoli to booths of Asian club kids pre–Ecstasy hit and average Joes mid–bar crawl. $20

Pagolac 655 Larkin St. (Ellis & Eddy Sts.) (415) 776-3234 Vietnamese. Hole in the wall, right down to Formica and linoleum. But the house specialty, seven courses of beef, is a winner—serious beef that means business. Lemongrass tofu, five-spice chicken, and build-your-own spring rolls, too. $10

Pho Hoa Vietnamese Restaurant 431 Jones St. (O'Farrell St.) (415) 673-3163 Vietnamese. Don't trip over the zonked-out guys clutching their Night Train, but don't let them scare you away, either. The pho is tops—get here early in the morning for an authentic Saigon breakfast. You'll be sharing a table with Vietnamese families, construction workers, and a few Nob Hill souls brave enough to make the trek. $10

Ponzu 401 Taylor St. (O'Farrell St.) (415) 775-7979 Asian Fusion. Nouveau Trader Vic's for South Bay types and tourists. Blue floors with dots, swirls, and checks not really a good idea. Oh well, just get in the mood with a Bruce Lychee, then work your way through chicken spring rolls and Chinese baby back ribs. $25

Ryoko Restaurant & Bar 619 Taylor St. (Post St.) (415) 775-1028 Sushi. After boozing it up proper in your buddy's room at the Clift, this'll fix that late-night spider-roll craving. Sushi chef Atsushi Matsuda even whips up soothing Japanese green-tea combo bowl to stave away the ache. Not much of a scene unless you count lovelorn guy weeping into his Sapporo, but open till 2 a.m. $25

Saigon Sandwich Shop 560 Larkin St. (Eddy St.) (415) 474-5698 Vietnamese Sandwiches. Little atmosphere and nowhere to sit, but Civic Center workers line up anyway. It's all about the banh mi on fresh warm French bread with shredded carrots, sprigs of cilantro, five-spice sauce and meatball pork, barbecue chicken, or pate. Don't shy away from gelatinous mystery substances in the cooler. $5 **BlackBook**

Sanraku 704 Sutter St. (Taylor St.) (415) 771-0803 Japanese. Bare-bones, but suits from Tokyo and local chefs don't mind the wait. In that sense, resembles actual Tokyo osushi-ya. Fresh-from-the-sea scallops and raw sweet shrimp, no better tempura any-where. Things aren't quite as hectic next door at its sedate sister, Four Seasons. +$25

Shalimar 532 Jones St. (O'Farrell St.) (415) 928-0333 Pakistani. Most devout fol-lowing of three Indian/Pakistani spots within spitting distance. Not the kind of place you'd bring yo' mama. Weird bleach smell means they must clean this joint, right? Oh well, at least the food's good. Watch guys bake naan and lamb chops in the blazing-hot tandoor as you order spicy-as-all-out bhuna gosht. $12

Slider's Diner 1202 Sutter St. (Polk St.) (415) 885-3288 American. Hustlers and queens next to Nob Hill 9-to-5s. Asian family that runs this place keeps it super-clean, from gleaming appliances to spotless bathrooms. Order your burger any way you like it, then grab your own toppings: shredded lettuce, sliced tomatoes, and onions, yes, but also bell peppers, olives, pepperoncini, and chickpeas. $10

Sun's Café 652 Polk St. (Eddy St.) (415) 776-9595 Korean/Japanese/American. Quintessential SF greasy spoon, with eggs and bacon, burgers and fries, and bul-gogi—say whaat? California Culinary Academy students in trainer togs nosh on BLTs or chicken teriyaki during lunch breaks. $7

Thai House Express 901 Larkin St. (Geary Blvd.) (415) 441-2248 Thai. Do-it-yourself Thai fare lets you mix and match ingredients. Soups are main attraction, with larb at the top of the list. Clean bathrooms, bit more upscale than Osha Thai Noodle down the street. $15

Tommy's Joynt 1101 Geary Blvd. (Van Ness Ave.) (415) 775-4216 German-American Cafeteria. The guys from Metallica used to hang at this neon-lit hofbrau before they were millionaires, and the look hasn't changed since. Turkey and roast beef carved to order for sandwiches, buffalo stew for buffalo gals, platters of sausages for guys watching the big game. $10

Vietnam II 701 Larkin St. (Ellis St.) (415) 885-1274 Vietnamese. For those nights when you just want to plonk at a table with a good book and a heap of comfort food. Huge bowl of pho with rare slices of beef to cook in steamy broth with rice noodles, cilantro, jalapenos, and chile sauce. Not the most stylish place in town, but consistently good. $10

Wrap Deli 426 Larkin St. (Golden Gate St.) (415) 771-3388 Vietnamese sandwiches. Like Saigon Sandwiches up the street, a hole-in-the-wall lunch takeout serving just one thing: banh mi sandwiches. This selection, from pork balls to fried tofu, blows its neighbor away. Array of packaged Vietnamese snacks will have you scratching your head for days. $5

NIGHTLIFE Tenderloin & Downtown

222 Club 222 Hyde St. (Turk St.) (415) 440-0222 Ambitious little spot for such gritty surroundings, but someone's got to do it. Owners transformed this washed-up dive by themselves, painting the interior bright-red and sanding down the bar. Short list of bites like tuna poke and garlic prawns to go with soju cocktails and wines by the glass.

Blur Cocktails & Sushi 1121 Polk St. (Post & Sutter Sts.) (415) 567-1918 Trendyish hangout amid the pawnshops. Sushi bar turns out creative little rolls (see Beach Boys with deep-fried banana) and unusually potent sake cocktails. The Blurry Dog will make you one blurry dawg, all right.

Café Royale 800 Post St. (Leavenworth St.) (415) 441-4099 Bastion of laid-back cool on corner of ho-hum block. Plush velvet couches, snazzy wine list, live jazz, rotating art, and decent bar food. Pool table where players who suck can shoot and not be embarrassed. Attractive artsy types in mellow pickup scene. Feels good in here.

Empire Plush Room Cabaret 940 Sutter St. (Hyde St.) (415) 885-2800 There's something kinda cool about the York Hotel, where Kim Novak's character stayed in Vertigo. Legend has it this cabaret opened during Prohibition, with secret maze-like entrance inside. Torch singers for drama geeks, flamboyant mood, Astaire-inspired gigs or classic show tunes. Weekend burlesque at the Va Va Voom Room, now that's what we're talking about.

Great American Music Hall 859 O'Farrell St. (Polk St.) (415) 885-0750 Since 1907, baby, so you know it means business. Former bordello serving up fast women and fast times. Now one of the best concert halls in town, with rococo balconies and a rockin' oak dance floor. Permission to tear it up! Granted.

Ha-Ra Club 875 Geary Blvd. (Larkin St.) (415) 673-3148 There are dive bars, and then there's the Ha-Ra. Here's the protocol, son: Order a few shots of Wild Turkey, chase 'em down with a Bud, and then stumble over to the video poker machine and challenge a red-in-the-face old-timer to a game. If pool's more your thing, there's a table along the faux brick-lined wall.

Hemlock Tavern 1131 Polk St. (Hemlock Alley) (415) 923-0923 Wannabe Jeff Tweedys chain-smoke on enclosed heated patio. Just shrink your T-shirt, don't wash your hair, and you'll fit right in. Live acts like The Ponies in back room where there's a cover. Up front, the bartenders pour G&Ts nice. Grab a paper bag of warm peanuts but drop your shells on the floor, or get reamed by the snarly chick behind the bar.

Kimo's 1351 Polk St. (Pine St.) (415) 885-4535 Strange dichotomy afoot. Surfboards and fishing nets mix with chrome and mirrors, plus faded beefcake pin-ups and rock 'n' blues jukebox. No matter, things tend to get blurry after a while. Blame the vicious Jack and Cokes, or the clash of genres in the divey upstairs club. One night it's hard-core drag cabaret, then heavy metal or ska. Show up in drag or fetishwear for a break on the cover, no matter who's headlining.

Lush Lounge 1092 Post St. (Polk St.) (415) 771-2022 It might take a while for the camo shorts–wearing bartender to mix your martini (he's too busy reenacting the dance-off from that Pat Benatar video), but he doles out shots to make up for the wait. The crowd, definitely gay, doesn't give a crap about what's trendy. You'll make a few new friends, even on your first visit.

Olive Bar 743 Larkin St. (O'Farrell & Geary Sts.) (415) 776-9814 Kate Spade–toting chicks on the prowl after work. Peals of laughter possibly a direct result of chocolate martinis. Thank goodness for thin-crust mushroom pizzas drizzled with truffle oil that keep things from getting too sloppy. Good date spot. Give the homeless guy some change on your way out.

Owl Tree 601 Post St. (Taylor St.) (415) 776-9344 Says the bartender: "If you got an owl in yer pocket, yer likely to get a free drink." For 27 years, folks round town have been enabling owner Bobby's insatiable owl habit, bringing him owl clocks, plates, cookie jars, assorted ornaments for his collection. Motley crew of drunken oldsters, decked-out hipsters, and Bobby's runty little dog. Jukebox kicks ass from Sinatra to Elvis, plus random musical soundtracks. **BlackBook**

R Bar 1176 Sutter St. (Polk St.) (415) 567-7441 Empty bottles of Fernet lining mahogany shelf above doorway should be clue number one. Bartenders gunning back Fernet shot after shot should be clue number two. Owners Tod and Chris love their jobs, and it shows. They're mixing business with pleasure, all right—not that there's anything wrong with that.

Red Room 827 Sutter St. (Jones & Leavenworth Sts.) (415) 346-7666 Tiny room where everything's red, from benches to throw pillows to bottles on the wall. Oh, except for the scrumptious female bartenders in sexy black ensembles. Mighty fine sidecars, budget-swank guests from Commodore Hotel.

Ruby Skye 420 Mason St. (Geary St.) (415) 693-0777 Shell out the C notes. Multilevel dance club with private smoking lounge and cigar bar, plus booth service that gives you VIP access and the chance to look like a baller. Hotties in halter tops, slicked-back suburban yahoos, and plenty of the cheaper Gucci milling about.

Rx Gallery 132 Eddy St. (Mason St.) (415) 474-7973 Permanent gallery/club of the cutting-edge Blasthaus collective, and one of the coolest underground spots in town. Rotating art installations, eclectic DJs off the Thievery Corp label, sci-fi happy hour to synth soundtracks. House-party vibe thanks to decks on the floor, hodgepodge of speakers, and fashionable little honeys getting down. Best intimate spot to hear the best music SF gets.**BlackBook**

suite one8one 181 Eddy St. (Taylor & Mason Sts.) (415) 345-9900 Don't be fooled by the area code. We're trying real hard to break away from the SF club scene, see? We got billowy white curtains like Miami, tramped-up hoochies like

L.A., generic cheesy house like we could be in Ibiza. Fellas in tight black Ts emanate VIP attitudes on dance floor and off.

Swig 561 Geary Blvd. (Taylor St.) (415) 931-7292 There goes the neighborhood. Used to be a rundown, gritty place to catch live bands. These days, it's looking more like a genteel bar. Almost makes us nostalgic for faint smell of urine that used to linger in the air. But fireplace and hand-blown light fixtures aren't bad. DJs spin usual blend of funk, hip-hop, and soul (yawn).

Who's Your Daddy? 655 Sutter St. (Mason St.) (415) 923-9090 Well, who is it? If the waitresses wore orange hot pants and owl T-shirts, you'd think this was Hooters. Bud Light in chilled mugs, plus TVs galore and dartboards for those running short on Ritalin. But can someone explain the members-only Chinese karaoke bar in back?

_____

_____

_____

_____

_____

_____

_____

_____

"Your city is remarkable not only for its beauty. It is also, of all the cities in the United States,

the one whose name, the world over, conjures up the most visions and more than any other,

incites one to dream. " —Georges Pompidou

NORTH BEACH, CHINATOWN & FISHERMAN'S WHARF (map p.116-117)

Heads up: **This is tourist territory, so get ready for the fannypack crush.** Like a greatest-hits medley on the SF musical tour, these three 'hoods have the densest concentration of postcard-ready attractions: phallic **Coit Tower**, lurid **Chinatown Gate**, chowder-centric **Pier 39**. So make like the locals, and you'll be just fine. **North Beach** is part beatnik, part louche, flaunting remnants of its Barbary Coast past in the garish red-light strip on Broadway. Sal and Vito exit the Italian Athletic Club and stop for focaccia at Liguria Bakery, as ripped chicks in cutoff shorts keep that volleyball in play in Washington Square Park. You might catch Papa Coppola holding court in his café, or Ferlinghetti keeping it real upstairs at **City Lights**. **Chinatown is full of coy discoveries**, like the steamy underground parties in Li Po's former opium den, or the six-course meal to die for at jewel-in-the-rough **Jai Yun**. Ahh, Chinatown: an excellent place to get plastered in the afternoon. (We're partial to **Grasslands** on Kearny, "Where Good Friends And Girls Meet.") As for Fisherman's Wharf, the barking sea lions sure are cute, but those endless T-shirt shops and crappy galleries are a buzzkill. Just concentrate on the good stuff: the cracked crab on the pier, the cheese cart at **Gary Danko**, and the audio tour at Alcatraz (that all-too-rare thing, the tourist trap that truly delivers). We'll meet you at the secret VIP room at **Tosca** and get our card game on before catching Kim Nalley at **Jazz at Pearl's** and Nouvelle Vague at **Bimbo's**.

RESTAURANTS North Beach, Chinatown & Fisherman's Wharf

Ana Mandara 891 Beach St. (Polk St.) (415) 771-6800 Modern Vietnamese. Peep the professional soundstage lighting across the ceiling? With founding owners Don Johnson and Cheech Marin, such Hollywood-flavored details are par for the course. Cordon Bleu-trained Chef Khai Duong makes this lavish Ghirardelli Sq. destination purr. Crispy lobster ravioli, tender Mekong basa, and lemongrass-infused Ana Mandara cocktails that go down way too easy. $45

Bocadillos 710 Montgomery St. (Washington St.) (415) 982-2622 Basque/Tapas. So it takes a lot of small plates to make a meal (which makes the prices bratty). And the wait can be tedious (unless you care to chill out at cheesy Bubble Lounge next door). But the True Religion-sporting couples fighting their way for a seat at the bar know what's up. Prada-pink Serrano ham, crunchy sardines, roasted pepper salad, staggering wine list. Sexy like you want it to be. So very Barcelona. +$35 **BlackBook**

Butterfly Pier 33, Embarcadero (Bay St.) (415) 291-9482 Cal-Asian Fusion. Sunset Strip on the Embarcadero. Beautiful people fronting like they don't give a damn. Stiff cocktails, rock-star lighting, live jazz, sweeping bay views. Duck confit spring rolls and Niman Ranch sizzling cowboy steak. A trip to LA, without the hassle of LAX. $4

Café Jacqueline 1454 Grant Ave. (Union St.) (415) 981-5565 Soufflés. Does only one thing, and does it damn well. Candlelit dining room and big windows radiate satisfying warmth and snugness. Play it safe with the classic gruyère soufflé, or walk on the wild side with the salmon-asparagus. For dessert, chocolate is where it's at. Remember, you can't hurry love: Soufflés are made to order, and they take their sweet-ass time. $35

Caffe Trieste 609 Vallejo St. (Grant & Columbus Aves.) (415) 392-6739 Coffeehouse. Half a century of bohemian history endows this coffeehouse with undeniable cred. Papa Gianni came over from the old country in 1951, kids and grandkids carry on tradition of brewing espresso that would make the Corleones proud. Packs them in come Saturday afternoons, when the entire Giotta clan pulls a von Trapp and warbles opera and show tune classics. They're feeling it. $12

Da Flora 701 Columbus Ave. (Filbert St.) (415) 981-4664 Venetian. Some places have style, but this place has soul. Dig the lush red décor and aromas wafting from the kitchen. Swoon-inducing sweet potato gnocchi, fall-off-the-bone lamb shank, great all-Italian wine list. $30

El Raigón 510 Union St. (Grant Ave.) (415) 291-0927 Argentine. Hereford cowhides stretched like canvas adorn brick walls at this temple to meat. Owners, who also run a working ranch in Argentina, clearly know their cow. Various cuts grilled parilla-style topped off with piquant chimichurri sauce. Wine list dominated by Argentine Malbecs and California micro-producers makes you realize they're onto something here. Round it out indulgently with the dulce de leche. $30

Golden Flower 667 Jackson St. (Grant Ave.) (415) 433-6469 Vietnamese. Word is out on this joint. Dirt-cheap, good-quality Vietnamese pho, rice noodles, and grilled meats served up by friendly folks who actually seem happy to be there. Lighting's fluorescent, and your table might not be pristine, but you'll overlook these minor glitches. Savory imperial rolls and succulent barbecue pork. Get there early for lunch on weekdays, as it fills up quick. $15

The Helmand 430 Broadway St. (Montgomery St.) 415-362-0641 Afghan. You'll need to negotiate Broadway's strip-club barkers to get here, but it's well worth the effort for this sleeper hit. Owner Mahmoud Karzai, brother of Afghan president Hamid, sure knows his pumpkin—the fried, then baked kaddo is not to be missed. Turkish coffee served tableside is fit for a warlord. $25

The House 1230 Grant Ave. (Columbus Ave.) (415) 986-8612 Cal-Asian Fusion. Neighborhood favorite for Saturday date night. You'll freak over the can-this-be-real flavor of the ginger-soy glazed sea bass, deep-fried salmon rolls, and crab cakes. Bit of a racket in the tight space, especially on weekends. $35

Il Fornaio 1265 Battery St. (Greenwich & Lombard Sts.) (415) 986-0100 Italian. Remember, it's not a chain, it's a "multi-location" establishment. Reliable, high-quality Italian standards, occasionally an inventive special or two, excellent housemade breads. Heavy on imported marble. Crowd of polished tourists and locals. $30

Iluna Basque 701 Union St. (Powell St.) (415) 402-0011 Basque tapas. Button-cute Basque golden boy Mattin Noblia keeps this place humming along nicely, serving up lush small plates in a dim, dark-paneled corner. Seared tuna on what has to be the most delicate cheese sauce ever. Sip on a Basque martini or the kick-ass gazpacho, served in a tumbler and chock-full of flavor. Good for an eight-course meal or a glass of French cider at the bar. $30

In-N-Out Burger 333 Jefferson St. (Jones St.) 800-786-1000 Fast Food. Believe the hype! America's first drive-thru chain gets simple, quick, heart-attack food right. The non-God-fearing among us may be put off by the religious quotes on the plastic cups, but the place still rocks. Ask for your burger "Animal Style," with a mustard-grilled bun, extra sauce, and lots of luscious grilled onions. They won't give you a weird look, we promise. $7

Jai Yun 923 Pacific Ave. (Mason St.) (415) 981-7438 Chinese. Chef Nei Chia-Ji stands apart, serving up stylized specialties from far-flung regions of China. Steady stream of dishes like velvet abalone and melt-in-your-mouth pork roast make this one of the best Chinese restaurants in town. Nothing in terms of atmosphere, but, trust us, you won't even notice. +$35 **BlackBook**

L'Osteria del Forno 519 Columbus Ave. (Green St.) (415) 982-1124 Tuscan. Best small Italian joint in North Beach. Waiting for one of 28 seats can be forever, and they don't take reservations. All is forgiven the second you bite into the thin-crust pizza, tender milk-braised pork roast, toasted focaccia sandwiches, or housemade pasta. Festive and boisterous, as old-timers and tourists revel in the bounty. $30

Mario's Bohemian Cigar Store and Cafe 566 Columbus Ave. (Union St.) (415) 362-0536 Italian. Picturesque old favorite right on Washington Square Park, proudly serving up crisp focaccia sandwiches, bubbling baked pasta, perfectly thin pizzas, and handmade biscotti. Add a cappuccino or smooth-drinking red wine to the mix. Bring a book and camp out for an afternoon. $15

Mama's on Washington Square 1701 Stockton St. (Filbert St.) (415) 362-6421 Breakfast. The place for morning grub in North Beach, with a ridiculously long line to prove it. Homemade cinnamon brioche, perfect omelets with exotic cheeses, eggs lightly scrambled with smoked salmon or fresh crab. Country-kitchen decor works, if only because you're so damned happy to finally be sitting down. $15

Maykadeh 470 Green St. (Grant Ave.) (415) 362-8286 Persian. Persian expat favorite for 20 years. Elegant, understated dining room just off chaotic corner of Grant and Green. Magnificent kebabs, basmati rice, and tender lamb. Real winner is the soltani, a hefty portion of skewer-grilled filet mignon marinated in lime juice and onion. Persian pistachio ice cream for dessert. $35

Mo's Gourmet Hamburgers 1322 Grant Ave. (Vallejo St.) (415) 788-3779 Highfalutin' diner. Ignore annoying Three Stooges design scheme and concentrate on excellent burger. Top-quality meat ground daily, with additions like gruyere cheese, thick smoky bacon, and caramelized onions. Hand-cut fries are nice, but red cabbage slaw is exceptional. $15

Myth 470 Pacific Ave. (Montgomery St.) (415) 677-8986 California-French. Moneyed SF blend of politicos, funky Nob Hill doyennes, Charles Schwab suits, Kate Spade corporate chicks, plus hussies at the bar. Eclectic design mélange turns exposed brick and gleaming wood into surprisingly cozy space. Food is sexy and indulgent, as in warm sweetbread salad with shiitakes. Sommelier fast becoming a legend. +$46 ★

Piperade 1015 Battery St. (Green St.) (415) 391-2555 Basque French. Style-forward Basque brasserie headed up by affable chef Gerald Hirigoyen, who mingles at length with every table. Refined, yet explosive flavors. Signature piperade—roasted tomatoes and peppers with Serrano ham and poached egg—and towering Dungeness crab salad. Excellent wine list, and perhaps the finest mojito in town. +$40

R&G Lounge 631 Kearny St. (Commercial St.) (415) 982-7877 Chinese. Nicely renovated Chinatown landmark where food goddess Alice Waters celebrated her birthday. Don't be spooked by Secret Service wires worn by the hosts. Just ask for a table in the upstairs dining room, and get the salt-and-pepper crab fresh out of the tank. $25

Restaurant Gary Danko 800 North Point St. (Hyde St.) (415) 749-2060 Contemporary American. Itching to drop some serious cash on a seriously unforgettable meal? Go here. From the exquisite amuse-bouche to the last drop of port, every detail is flawless. Understated dining room, staff that predicts your every need, a connoisseur's wine list, cheese course for the gods. Plan on spending a small fortune, and reserve well in advance. $45

Rose Pistola 532 Columbus Ave. (Union St.) (415) 399-0499 Italian. Proof you can be the hottest restaurant in town and still be around five years later. Rose Pistola has triumphed, against the odds. Snag a sidewalk table on warm days and share plentiful antipasti, the freshest fish anywhere, or the "terrorized" New York steak. $40

Sodini's 510 Green St. (Grant Ave.) (415) 291-0499 Italian. This place was calling itself a trattoria before anyone else in this country knew what that meant. Basic, mom-and-pop Italian-American comfort food: veal piccata, spaghetti and meatballs, tossed green salad, garlic bread. Decor hasn't been updated in decades, which is nice, because Chianti-bottle candleholders covered in wax drippings are kinda cool. $30

Tommaso's 1042 Kearny St. (Broadway St.) (415) 398-9696. Classic Italian. Who says there's no good pizza in San Francisco? Oak-fired brick oven cranks out some of the tastiest thin-crust pies anywhere. Consistent Italian-American comfort food like fried calamari, meaty lasagna, and veal parmigiana served up with pasta. Bit of a wait on weekends, but worth it once you get down to business. $20

NIGHTLIFE North Beach, Chinatown & Fisherman's Wharf

15 Romolo 15 Romolo Pl. (Broadway St.) (415) 398-1359 Welcome sigh of relief amid generic beer halls and pickup joints. Dim lighting, excellent indie-heavy jukebox, well-made drinks keep locals and in-the-know visitors satisfied. Hip without flaunting it, swanky but not overdone. Weekends find the medium-sized room packed, weekdays quiet enough for conversation.

Bimbo's 365 Club 1025 Columbus Ave. (Chestnut St.) (415) 474-0365 Top-flight indie, soul, and jazz acts in swanked-out venue devoid of attitude. Glamorous 1931 mainstay where Rita Hayworth once kicked up her gams. Bartenders wear tuxedoes, and red velvet drapes the walls, but civility rules and the crowd plays nice. **BlackBook**

Buena Vista Café 2765 Hyde St. (Beach & North Point Sts.) (415) 474-5044 Irish coffee's American birthplace where locals go to feel like tourists. Even in the shadow of tacky Fisherman's Wharf, this place has soul to spare. Opened for business in 1916. Claims to serve up to 2,000 boozy coffee treats a day, so have at least one, for tradition's sake.

Blend 659 Columbus Ave. (Filbert St.) (415) 296-7879 Polynesian-flavored hepcat hangout featuring—you guessed it—blended cocktails. Promises tropical bliss and delivers. Drink your way around the cocktail menu as you drift into a frosty alternate reality. Groovy funk on the sound system leads the way.

Empress of China Cocktail Lounge 838 Grant Ave (Washington & Clay Sts.) (415) 434-1345 Lost in Translation meets suburban Holiday Inn. Seldom what you'd call a scene, but don't let that stop you. Impressive cineaste-worthy views. Meet friends for the first drink of the night, or wander into roof-garden restaurant for pleasantly greasy dumplings.

Enrico's 504 Broadway St. (Kearny St.) (415) 982-6223 Excellent live jazz and swinging streetside patio with ideal North Beach vantage point. Amazingly effective heat lamps ensure keep nippy San Francisco nights at bay. Bartenders know how to muddle their mojitos. Top-notch food as well.

EZ5 682 Commercial St. (Kearny St.) (415) 362-9321 Oddly located, intriguing spot packed with the kind of kitsch (beanbags, Bruce Lee posters) you'd find in a split-level rec room. Electro-rock on turntables and archival videos projected on back wall add comfortable house-party feel. Home to finance types, Chinatown-chic, lost tourists, and folks seeking North Beach alternative.

Fuse 493 Broadway St. (Kearny St.) (415) 788-2706 Sparkly-blue watering hole and DJ spot known for tiny yet inviting dance floor. More of Mission vibe than typical North Beach. Friendly bartenders ply you with potent creations like the Cucumber Cosmopolitan. Rarely a cover.

Jazz at Pearl's 256 Columbus Ave. (Broadway St.) (415) 291-8255 Storied supper club rescued from oblivion and better than ever. Come Tuesday nights, catch owner and knockout jazz crooner Kim Nalley, who sure can fill out a sequined dress. Serious jazz lovers here—that means no talking over the music. Food can be decent, surprisingly. **BlackBook**

Li Po 916 Grant Ave. (Washington St.) (415) 982-0072 Bad lighting, Buddha statue, red vinyl booths at this Chinatown mainstay. No karaoke here, but a bare-bones performance space in the basement, supposedly a former opium den, hosting miniscule rock acts and the occasional impromptu mod party. Beer served in plastic cups is drink of choice, and MJ circa "Thriller" is the musical backdrop. It is what it is, and we like it.

Magnet 1402 Grant Ave. (Green St.) (415) 271-5760. There's only so many things you can do with sake and soju, and these guys have figured out every last one of them. Sleek decor, snug space, mysterious Russian owners lend an air of danger and possibility. Young, inoffensive, non-frat types predominate.

Mr. Bing's 201 Columbus Ave. (Pacific St.) (415) 362-1545 Must be the V-shaped bar. Tiny, unassuming tavern, formerly just a dive, now next big divey thing. Cute girls and boys order Buds and screwdrivers with well vodka. Specter of bona-fide hipness lurks.

Rosewood 732 Broadway St. (Stockton & Powell Sts.) 415-951-4886 Unmarked door and shuttered windows conceal out-of-the-way, slightly more gussied-up relation to 15 Romolo. Hot, young, Hoegaarden-drinking crowd on black leather sofas, chair-dancing to saucy French hip-hop.

The Saloon 1232 Grant Ave. (Vallejo St.) (415) 989-7666 Still sleazy after all these years. San Francisco's oldest drinkery, with 140 years of infamy. Regulars of this whisky 'n' blues joint wear the name Saloonatics as a badge of honor. Not a place to hook up, but you may find yourself a deal on a vintage Harley. Behave.

Specs' 12 Adler St. (Broadway St. & Pacific Ave.) (415) 421-4112 Dark, beatniky, root-cellar feel. Check the 'tude at the door or find yourself out on your ass. Earnest youngsters and older intellectuals in animated, brainy conversation. Drink beer, not cocktails. If you must order a Grey Goose cosmo, be prepared for a roll of the eyes and a weary sigh from a bartender who's seen North Beach change too much over the years.

Suede 383 Bay St. (Mason St.) (415) 399-9555 So this is where they find all those pharmaceutical-sales chicks on The Bachelor. Get past a somewhat stiff crowd (were those pleated khakis?) and it kicks in pretty well, actually. Candle-heavy lighting, plush couches, four bars and multiple levels assure you can always find a drink. The signature Rastini cocktail is worthy. Music, mainly generic deep house and radio hip-pop can be quite good when drunk.

Tony Niks 1534 Stockton St. (Green St.) (415) 693-0990 Updated retro-classy juke joint the Rat Pack would have loved. Snag a seat at the long bar or hustle into a back table and commence conspiratorial mutterings. Cocktail-friendly bartenders pour drinks that pack a punch. Crowd of locals and off-duty restaurant staff keep the good times rolling.

Tosca 242 Columbus Ave. (Broadway St.) (415) 986-9651 Pinnacle of North Beach chic, especially if you can find your way into the cloistered back room. Unless you pal about with Sean Penn or Francis Ford, don't count on it. Bask with the minions in conversational roar of mural-lined barroom. Pop a quarter in the opera-dominated vinyl jukebox and drink your sidecar in style. **BlackBook**

Vesuvio Caffe 255 Columbus Ave. (Broadway St.) (415) 362-3370 Get loaded where Kerouac did! Legendary beatnik watering hole that's retained its soul. Tourists come and go; neighborhood insiders make the place what it is. Knock back a beer at a tiny upstairs table at midnight or 6 a.m. while you scribble a letter to a faraway friend.

"The San Francisco Bay Area: the playpen of countercultures." —R. Z. Sheppard

RUSSIAN HILL & NOB HILL (map p. 118)

Think of these neighborhoods as make-out central. Views, views, and more views for the taking—so much sensory overload it feels chemically induced. We're in **Russian Hill, home to all those sappy SF clichés that still manage to win you over.** Shingled homes, cable cars, glowing bistros, you get the picture. Tour this 'hood on foot—it's well worth the calf burn. Before Wisteria Lane, there was Barbary Lane; peep the real-life version at pedestrian-only Macondray. And if you're gonna drive the so-called crookedest street in the world (even though any SF-er can tell you Potrero's Vermont takes the honors), do it at night when the locals do. Upper Polk's got the usual boutiques and boulangeries and a hard-drinking, bar-hopping crowd, less annoying by far than the Marina's. (A 2 a.m. run to Bob's Donuts soaks up the Fernet something proper.) **Nob Hill is a bit more on the Upper East Side tip**, with its massive Grace Cathedral and wedding-cake hotels. It's all thanks to four big ballers who bankrolled the railroad and then bought up the neighborhood. Wear your pinky ring and bring your best girl—this is where we swing, baby. We'll be chowdering down counterside at **Swan Oyster Depot**, ogling the wine list at **1550 Hyde**, doing the tiki torch thing at the **Tonga Room**, and living the high life at the **Top of the Mark**.

RESTAURANTS Russian Hill & Nob Hill

The Big Four 1075 California St. (Taylor St.) (415) 771-1140 American. The true definition of old school. Gents with pinky rings in coat and tie, dames with coiffed dos and pearls. Named after four railroad tycoons who blazed a trail back in the day. Darkly lit ambiance with clubby banquettes, wild game dishes like ostrich or buffalo. A keeper. +$45 **BlackBook**

Boulange de Polk 2308 Polk St. (Green & Union Sts.) (415) 345-1107 French Bakery/Cafe. So authentic, all that's missing is the smoke. Expats sitting outside savoring home-baked quiches and pastries with bottomless bowls of latte. Nibble now or pack in a picnic basket for later. Dark and crusty cannelés de Bordeaux, croque monsieur with side of cornichons. You love Paris in the springtime. $10

1550 Hyde 1550 Hyde St. (Pacific Ave.) (415) 775-1550 Californian. Seasonality taken to dazzling new heights. Faro and corn-stuffed quail, polenta-almond cake with organic strawberries and cream, kickass wine list to boot. You're toasted on the Cab, room is aglow with warmth and cheer, you're loving life and the people you're with. Good times. +$35

Frascati 1901 Hyde St. (Green St.) (415) 928-1406 Cal-Med. You must remember this. Romantic corner spot with wine-centric menu and seasonal cuisine. Lovely floral arrangements, country-kitchen feel and tucked-away upstairs tables. Table 21 is batting 1,000 for marriage proposals. We'll always have Frascati. $40

Habana 2080 Van Ness Ave. (Pacific Ave & Jackson St.) (415) 441-2822 Cuban. Cuba, circa 1948, minus the cars, mobsters, and Papa Hemingway. Instead, we're talking banana palms, jaguar mural, silk-draped pavilion. Start with seasonal ceviche and picadillo before blissing out on seafood paella. Sweet Cuba Libres and Latin jazz make for hot, sultry Havana nights. $35

Harris' Steak House 2100 Van Ness Ave. (Pacific Ave.) (415) 673-1888 Steakhouse. Organic my ass. Sometimes all you want is a thick slab of dry-aged beef. No concessions to nouvelle cuisine here; spinach is creamed, martinis are stiff, and beef is the star of the show. Japanese businessmen and suburban couples out for that annual treat. $60

Luella 1896 Hyde St. (Green St.) (415) 674-4343 Cal-Med. Banana Republic casting call meets sleek, organic-chic eatery. Will it be Botox or Bordeaux tonight? Wines by the glass, chartreuse banquettes, lowlit ambience makes for girls-night-out glow. Bone marrow butter and Coca-Cola braised pork shoulder should clue you in to not very Karl Lagerfeld–sized portions. Two words: ricotta fritters. $35 ★

Nick's Crispy Tacos 1500 Broadway (Polk St.) (415) 409-8226. Mexican. Chef-owner Nick rents out space from nightclub impresario Harry Denton. Thus the Mexican ponchos over plush velvet booths and supersized piñatas clinging to pricey chandeliers. Crispy-shelled taco stuffed with wild salmon or beer-battered mahi-mahi, then double-wrapped in a soft shell for a wham-bam-thank-you-ma'am treat. $8

Nob Hill Café 1152 Taylor St. (Clay St.) (415) 776-6500 Italian. Hey Vito, is my car ready? Comfortable neighborhood classic with endless bowls of spaghetti alla carbonara, gnocchi bolognese, lasagna, and some garlic bread to bring it all home. Bensonhurst by way of Nob Hill. $28

Pasha 1516 Broadway (Polk St. & Van Ness Ave.) (415) 885-4477 Middle Eastern. Paging Aladdin and Scheherazade. Over-the-top Disney set with every imaginable Arabian Nights cliché. Ornate wall murals, beanbag cushions, tapestries and carpets from Azerbaijan. Live music, waiters sporting fezes, and belly dancing to standards like hummus, lamb kebab, and mint tea. So cheesy it hurts. $35

Rex Cafe 2323 Polk St. (Union & Green Sts.) (415) 441 2244 Bistro. High-ceilinged, saloon-styled spot with fading streams of sunlight and lazy fans circling dreamily overhead. Gorilla Sports sends young, healthy set over for post-workout mimosas. 83-year-old Mareva balances it out. Standard California bistro, special touches like pineapple-infused vodka and wide range of tequilas. Brunch the way it oughta be. Viva la Rex. $25

Street 2141 Polk St. (Broadway & Vallejo Sts.) (415) 775-1055 Global Californian. Will and Grace and their buddies talk current events at the corner window. Charming feel-good den feeds friends and neighbors. Sit at the bar, drink house-infused vodka, and watch burly John Lamkin make magic with simple ingredients. Melt-in-your-mouth potato dumplings, Sunday night buttermilk fried chicken. Skip the skinny jeans.

Sushi Groove 1916 Hyde St. (Union & Green Sts.) (415) 440-1905 Japanese. Downtempo edamame. Club royalty Martel & Nabiel's original excursion. Warm golden tones and quiveringly fresh fish make this the grooviest sushi indeed. Feel the force of the samurai chefs with sublime miso-marinated cod. Amberjack sashimi turns your tongue into a magic carpet ride. Nigiri with night-out aesthetic. $35

Swan Oyster Depot 1517 Polk St. (Sacramento & California Sts.) (415) 673-1101 Seafood. Tiny, no-nonsense, and bursting at the gills with the freshest seafood, ever since 1912. Motley assortment of lunchers, from socialites to Hell's Angels, lining up on sidewalk for one of 22 counter seats. Be dazzled by the non-stop shucking, shelling and fileting of the Sancimino brothers, who serve up your crab louie or clam chowder with a down-home smile. $22 **BlackBook**

Swensen's Ice Cream Parlor 1999 Hyde St. (Union St.) (415) 775-6818 Ice Cream. Gee Mr. Swensen, your ice cream sure tastes swell. '50s nostalgic parlor. Homemade caramel turtle fudge and sticky chewy chocolate, waffle cones baked on the spot and a nice picture of the man himself to let you know who to thank for it all. Original location, opened in 1948. Nowhere to sit and lick, so get a carton or two to go. Not just for the kiddies. $5

Tablespoon 2209 Polk St. (Vallejo St.) (415) 268-0140 New American. Former Spoon gets an upgrade, keeps teaspoon-sized space. Cool and casual joint stays open later—rare blessing in SF. Short rib ravioli, unctuous mac and cheese, Liberty duck breast sets things up nicely. Wines are "Fast and Easy," "Supple and Round," "Earthy and Animalistic." We like. $41 ✮

U-Lee 1468 Hyde St. (Jackson St.) (415) 771-9774 Cantonese. Some of the best pot stickers in the world: fat and full, pan-fried crispy and doughy good. Business-card testimonials to prove it. Clean and surprisingly un-greasy, fresh veggie dishes packing a crunch. Total treasure. $14

Yabbies Coastal Kitchen 2237 Polk St. (Green & Vallejo Sts.) (415) 474-4088 Seafood. Floor-to-ceiling chalkboard menu, raw bar covered with heaps o' crab legs waiting to be cracked, bevy of oysters poised for shucking. Nightly regulars welcomed on a first-name basis, lone diners enveloped like a clam in a shell. $40

Za Pizza 1919 Hyde St. (Union & Green Sts.) (415) 771-3100 Pizzeria. Gen X version of Big Chill. Hangout place stripped down to basics. Creedence and the Giants game. Friendly family hole-in-the-wall with warm oven smells and monthly art exhibitions. Thin and crispy crust, special combos such as Da Vinci's Palette and Pesto Picasso. Informal dinner or reliable last-minute standby. $10

Zarzuela 2000 Hyde St. (Union St.) (415) 346-0800 Spanish. Not quite late-night tapas in Seville, but it tries. Garlic, garlic, garlic—can you handle it? Chef/owner from Madrid, and from the looks of things a fan of the bullfights. Paella à la Valenciana washing down well with a refreshing mug of sangria. $27

NIGHTLIFE Russian Hill & Nob Hill

Bacchus 1954 Hyde St. (Union & Green Sts.) (415) 928-2633 Shoebox-sized wine and sake bar that serves as Sushi Groove waiting room. Just enough space for you and seven of your friends. Impressive specialty cocktails and international wine list focused on bou-tique vineyards. Loveseats by the window, West Village ambiance. Magical. **BlackBook**

Bigfoot Lounge 1750 Polk St. (Washington & Clay Sts.) (415) 440-2355 Paul Bunyan meets Smokey the Bear. Lowlit log cabin that's a full-tilt four-wheel-drive frontier for adults. Strange taxidermied creatures like the elusive jackalope and giant fake grizzly heads adorn the be-wooded walls. Tattooed hipsters and gruff old-timers, fake forest fire burning calmly over the bar. **BlackBook**

Cinch Saloon 1723 Polk St. (Clay St.) (415) 776-4162 Pinball, pool tables, and gay boys galore often leave this place SRO. Long, narrow Southwest-themed bar with bears, queens, and everything in between. Weekend barbecues on the out-door patio, $3 PBRs, '80s dance hits. Older crowd prefers muscle shirts, denim shorts, and Timberlands to Diesel, but everyone's just looking for a good time.

Harry Denton's Rouge 1500 Broadway (Polk St.) (415) 346-7683   B&T Bordello. Strip-club-meets-Moulin-Rouge décor. Velvet booths, mirrored walls, chandeliers. Tammy and her San Jose girlfriends making a special trip for her bachelorette party. Greasy predators, cheesy Euros and beefcake Asian studmasters negotiating for real estate on the dance floor.

Laurel Court 950 Mason St. (California & Sacramento Sts.) (415) 772-5260 Glide like a '40s movie star through the marbled lobby of the Fairmont Hotel. Handsome armchairs next to small wooden tables, cloistered corner couches conspiring with richly tapestried throw pillows, gorgeous deco lamps looming overhead. Crème brulée martini, signature San Francisco class.

N'Touch 1548 Polk St. (California & Sacramento Sts.) (415) 441-8413 There's something to be said for the city's only Asian gay bar. Trannies, hot-bodied go-go dancers, karaoke… these boys know how to throw a party. Dirt-cheap happy-hour prices don't hurt, either. If you're more Tom Cruise than Priscilla Queen of the Desert, pool tables are in back.

Nob Hill Tavern 1390 California (Hyde & Leavenworth Sts.) (415) 673-9294 In a sporty mood? Grab a frosty brew and work out your aggression with a nice round of pinball, a rousing game of foosball, or just yell like a good spectator at any of the six screens showing all sports all the time. Regular working-class fellas flesh out the early crowd, younger and more rowdy set arrive later to whoop it up.

Red Devil Lounge 1695 Polk St. (Clay St.) (415) 447-4730 Anne Rice ambiance from the red velvet curtains to the black iron staircase to the oversize chandelier. Oozes Gothic, but booking agent's penchant for '80s cover bands attract young BMW owners like bees to honey. Live music almost nightly, from local rock bands like Thistle to Sir Mix-A-Lot. T

Ritz-Carlton Bar 600 Stockton St. (California & Pine Sts.) (415) 296-7465 The lush life. Oversized stuffed chairs welcome rich and weary as they sip from snifters of brandy and wait for the help to bring the Bentley around. Crystal chandeliers, roaring fire, live pianist of course.

Royal Oak 2201 Polk St. (Green & Vallejo Sts.) (415) 928-2303 Victorian décor with '70s cheese atmo. The Regal Beagle to Russian Hill locals. Fruity Tiffany lamps, rich wood details, velvety couches, voluptuous barmaids. Just us regular folk. Sink into a stool, breathe the potted fern-enhanced oxygen, and decompress after a hard day of whatever it is you do.

Shanghai Kelly's 2064 Polk St. (Broadway) (415) 771-3300 In the 1870s, young fellers needed to beware of the infamous Shanghai Kelly, for he would spike yer drink and next thing you know you'd wake up on a merchant ship bound for China. Testosterone-soaked dive where bartenders are happy to retell the story, yet also proudly report the 52 marriages that have resulted from meetings within these walls.

The Tonga Room 950 Mason St. (Sacramento & California Sts.) (415) 772-5278 Unlikely portal into the South Seas, amid understated elegance of the Fairmont. Bring your insect repellent to the tropical island of kitsch. Teak wood tables, thatched roofs, rain machine. Top 40 cover band rocks the boat while afloat in the hotel's old swimming pool. Grab a Singapore Sling or Bora Bora Horror during happy hour and get good and greasy with the all-you-can-keep-down wonton-oriented buffet.

Tonic 2360 Polk St. (Union & Green Sts.) (415) 771-5535 Dark, narrow bar seeks NY vibe and LA crowd. Strong enough drinks that you'll start scarfing the complimentary gummy bears. Bartender moonlights as florist, hence the enormous arrangement. Friendly mix of giggling Marina girls and off-duty dads. Jukebox has it all: Al Green, Blur, and dash of the '80s for those who never got enough.

Top of the Mark 999 California St. (Mason St.) (415) 616-6916 On the 19th floor of the Mark Hopkins Hotel, glass-walled cocktail lounge with best views in town. Sip swankily on one of 100 different martinis and watch the sun descend upon the horizon. Wednesday nights brings such fun as salsa lessons with Benny Velarde and his Supercombo or the Black Market Jazz Orchestra on the weekend. Gussied-up revelers cutting a rug on elevated stage.

Tunnel Top 601 Bush St. (Mason St. & Grant Ave.) (415) 986-8900 Revived ex-Korean gambling bar that's hard to ignore, smack atop Stockton Tunnel and next to infamous Green Door massage parlor. Bartender Justin takes pride in his slow martini—don't rush him as he gently caresses the gin with turgid cubes of ice. International crowd with universal love for good times.

Zeki's Bar 1319 California St. (Hyde & Leavenworth Sts.) (415) 928-0677 Youngish crowd, healthy-looking and pre-jaded, happily enjoying pints of beer and swaying to fluffy sounds of Bob Marley, Van Morrison, and the Eagles. Pool table and friendly girlie bartender wearing a wifebeater and calling you honey. No pretensions, just drinking and forgetting.

SOMA & POTRERO HILL *(map p. 119)*

Once upon a time, there was a neighborhood called South of Market, bursting at the seams with arrogant baby millionaires, live/work lofts, and stratospheric stock options. It might seem like a fairy tale, but it was just five years ago. Much of **SoMa** is a Proustian lesson in the remembrance of things past: The once-cool club scene, which went off nightly with fresh new beats, fierce drag queens, and 24-hour party people, has been replaced by a painful bridge & tunnel set twirling their glowsticks to passé trance, or Burning Man types doing their best to keep a weeklong party on the playa a year-round Bay Area festivity. **The reckless spending and balls-out glory of the dot-com days are all but forgotten, but the kids still know how to party**, and the **EndUp** still personifies SF: diverse characters with sweet spirits and a healthy dose of naiveté. Ask any true SF-er and they'll tell you: The money was fun, but the cred is better. As for **Potrero Hill**, sure it borders the ghetto (a.k.a. O.J.'s original stompin' grounds), but this sunny land of hilly streets sports some of the best views and weather in town. No wonder it's where the Mission funky boys take their freaky girls to settle down. And while some of them hate to admit it, they all love to dine at the French mafia's trifecta: **Chez Papa**, **Chez Maman**, and **Baraka**, a sweet slice of suburban pie. It's certainly not the cheap and hidden gem it was a few years ago, but Potrero's still on the rise. Those hip to the next real estate boom are heading south to China Basin, still an industrial wasteland with the promise of good times to come. We've got a table at **Zuppa** and cocktails at **Lingba** with a disco nap before our 6 a.m. wake-up call for Darren Emerson at the **EndUp**.

RESTAURANTS SoMa & Potrero Hill

Aperto 1434 18th St. (Connecticut St.) (415) 252-1625 Italian. What we all want in our own neck of the woods. Go on a date, take your parents, interview a potential roommate over dinner. Sweet pea ricotta ravioli and coriander shrimp so succulent you won't mind waiting for a table. Crammed space, sweet service. $25

AsiaSF 201 9th St. (Howard St.) (415) 255-2742 Asian. Holy Asian gender bender! Like Lucky Cheng's, without the kitsch. Bachelorette parties and curiously creepy middle-aged dudes gawking at supple, well-endowed waitresses lip-syncing atop the bar on the hour. Food's decent, too: tamarind chicken satays and sake-steamed mussels. Not cheap, but the show is worth it. $40

Azie 826 Folsom St. (4th & 5th Sts.) (415) 538-0918 Asian Fusion. Bi-level dot-com leftover still chugging along, if a bit dated in concept and decor. Giant pagoda as mezzanine with crimson lanterns and curtained booths. Downtempo on the decks, tea-smoked quail on your plate, early-20somethings showing off for their dates. Nostalgia for 1999 running rampant, with or without Prince soundtrack. $45

Bacar 448 Brannan St. (4th St.) (415) 904-4100 Mediterranean. Tri-level pantheon of wine. Devoted cultists still come for spectacular list, but financially challenged masses can't afford it anymore. Vegas-like glass cellar of vino against lofty exposed brick depicts better times. Osso buco and pancetta wrapped quail still hold forth. $50

Baraka 288 Connecticut St. (18th St.) (415) 255-0387 Moroccan. Tiny Potrero Hill jewel glowing with candlelight and warm pumpkin walls. Moroccan, Spanish, and French cuisines superbly intermingled. Cabrales- and chorizo-stuffed dates and grilled squid, plus melt-in-your-mouth braised veal cheek tagine. Rose-scented martini as yummy as it sounds. Deep red lounge with low tables and velvet pillows. $40 **BlackBook**

Big Nate's Barbecue 1665 Folsom St. (12th St. & S. Van Ness Ave.) (415) 861-4242 Barbecue. Hole in the wall near freeway off-ramp owned by NBA Hall of Famer Nate Thurmond, who was a stud back when the Warriors were good. Known for smoky-flavored Memphis pulled pork. Place itself has little soul, just a counter, couple of tables, bare walls. Best to take out or hold out for free delivery on Saturdays and Sundays. $15

The Butler and the Chef 155 South Park St. (415) 896-2075 French. Delectable parkside bistro that's a little slice of Paris. Sit inside to avoid posse of bums with blaring disco boomboxes enjoying South Park shade. Cane-backed chairs, copper pots, vintage posters, the whole Gallic shebang. Flirty waiters dishing out charcuterie platters and croque-monsieurs, but of course. +$20

Canton Seafood & Dim Sum Restaurant 655 Folsom St. (2nd St.) (415) 495-3064 Chinese. Massive live seafood tank in busy, open dining room. Brass and crystal chandeliers, red Asian accents. Good place for cheap n' tasty dim sum or 12-course Chinese wedding banquet. Barbecue pork buns and fried taro root send you spiraling into a food coma. $25

Chez Maman 1453 18th St. (Missouri St.) (415) 824-7166 French. Don't let size fool you. Fabulous French for less than big brother Chez Papa up the street. Slide up to the counter or grab one of the two tables if you're lucky. Baked camembert with roasted garlic, signature crepe, burger topped with Roquefort and served with perfect frites. $25

Chez Papa 1401 18th St. (Missouri St.) (415) 255-0387 French. Cornerstone of 18th Street dining strip. Chic, bustling, sliver-sized bistro with some of the best Provencal dishes in town. Pastis-marinated prawns and pan bagnat joining luscious grilled figs with goat cheese at zinc-topped tables against Burgundy-colored walls. Reservations a must. $40

Coco500 500 Brannan St. (Fourth St.) (415) 543-2222 Cal-Med. French corner bistro gets fresh paint job and Scando-moderne interior, loses the tablecloths, and voila! Where you go to get your beef cheek mole on a chip. Da ex-Mayor Willie Brown, captains of industry, and assorted social demigods boisterously fraternizing amid Thonet seats and tight teak tables. Keep that bottarga coming, and choose death by decadent Cocobar. $42 ★

Goat Hill Pizza 300 Connecticut St. (18th St.) (415) 641-1440 Pizzeria. Of course a true SF pizza would have sourdough crust. Homemade tomato sauce, generous amounts of meat and veggies justify lines out the door. Cheap pitchers of SF's own Anchor Steam brewed right down the block. Red-checkered tablecloths, all-you-can-eat pizza-and-salad special on Mondays. Park it in back room for amazing skyline views. $20

Hawthorne Lane 22 Hawthorne Lane (Howard St.) (415) 777-9779 Californian. Not the newest or coolest kid on the block, but it works. Impeccable service, well-run bar, bathrooms as big as living rooms. Remarkably quiet despite large, open dining area. California cuisine with Asian flair: silky foie gras and uni with pasta bursting with flavor. $50

Jack Falstaff 598 Second St. (Brannan St.) (415) 836-9239 New American/Mediterranean. Avocado mousse–hued playroom for Gavin Newsom and his cultured cohorts. Liberal leanings meet old-boy clubby vibe (as in padded walls and suede banquettes). Meritage-swilling crowd gorging on decadent menu built on naughty organic food pyramid. That's right, pork belly cooked for 48 hours. $50 ★

Just for You Café 732 22nd St. (3rd St.) (415) 647-3033 American. Cozy institution composed mainly of hungover locals, due to remote Dogpatch location. Breakfast like ma used to make, served all day. Mind-boggling selection running the gamut from Hangtown Fry and crab cakes to breakfast burritos and beignets. Fresh bread baked on-site daily. $15

Le Charm 315 5th St. (Folsom St.) (415) 546-6128 French. True to its name, quaint French bistro makes you forget you're in SoMa. Lace curtains, warm yellow walls, back patio decorated with tiny white lights and climbing ivy. Well-priced prix-fixe (three courses for $25) starring gruyere-laden onion soup. $30

Maya 303 2nd St. (Folsom St.) (415) 543-2928 Mexican. Definitely not your local taqueria. Carved wooden doorways, rustic iron chandeliers, burnt orange walls. Tangy mahi-mahi ceviche and sweet pork quesadillas, ay caramba! Popular with business lunches, but in the land of Cesar Chavez, locals balk at high prices. Easily the fanciest Mexican joint in town—not always a good thing. $40

Mochica 937 Harrison St. (Fifth St.), (415) 278-0480 Peruvian. Sleeper ceviche bar of the year. Who needs atmo when you've got food this soulful, spicy, and affordable? So what if the look is circa 1992 and the view is a bunch of EndUp tweakers making a beeline for Blow Buddies. Oversized platters of Incan goodness spill forth, and all is forgiven. Pastel de camarones comes with strangely addictive Peruvian giant corn, while skewers of grilled beef heart satisfy the warrior in you. -$30 ★

Oola 860 Folsom St. (Fourth St.) 415-995-2061 American. We'll film the illicit tryst scene here. Sheer scarlet curtains, candlelight, orchids placed just so. Late-night schmancy comfort food for up-all-night Euro crowd in sexy split-level space. Chicken-and-foie-gras ravioli, just like Mom never made. Exposed brick backdrop, exposed skin on display. Ooh la la. $35 ★

Primo Patio Café 214 Townsend St. (3rd St.) 415-957-1129 Caribbean. Like being in someone's backyard across from the ballpark. Narrow corridor leads to back deck where pre-game fans chug sangria and "boulis boulis" pitchers. Quirky waitstaff led by affable hubby n' wife doling out cheap Caribbean eats like blackened snapper pitas and jerk chicken. Don't take more than one Tootsie Pop on the way out. $15

The Public Restaurant and Bar 1489 Folsom St. (11th St.))415) 552-3065 American. Gorgeous brick building that's more Tribeca than SoMa. Loft-like warehouse space warmed up by cozy décor and scrumptious Northern California cuisine. Is that lingerie on the lampshades? Cool kids converge on worn leather couches amid oversized art and exposed pipes. If the chocolate bread pudding can't make you happy, nothing will. $30

Restaurant LuLu 816 Folsom St. (4th St.) (415) 495-5775 French. Don't panic if you see flames. Popular restaurant known for enormous wood-burning oven in exhibition kitchen. Roasted mussels and fennel-scented pork loin. Roar of fire (and crowd) only enhanced by lofty wood-beamed ceiling. If you care about conversation, get a side booth. $35

Roe 651 Howard St. (2nd & 3rd Sts.) (415) 227-0288 Burmese-French-Japanese. Is it a restaurant? a nightclub? a terrifying amalgamation of the two? Two floors, two kinds of music, five kinds of caviar. Brick walls covered with gold drapery, long leopard-print bar, tulle hanging from ceiling. Hooray for more small plates—you eat them faster when you're uncomfortable. Maybe five years too late. $40

Shanghai 1930 133 Steuart St. (Mission St.) (415) 896-5600 Chinese. Classy Far East speakeasy, quiet and tasteful. Wide carpeted staircase leading down to low-ceilinged dining area. Remarkable shanghai dumpling appetizers, but entrees not worth the price. Stick to apps and drinks, enjoy live jazz, do dinner elsewhere. $50

South Park Café 108 South Park St. (Jack London Alley) (415) 495-7275 French. On picturesque South Park green. Crisp white tablecloths, sunny yellow walls, sidewalk tables, salty salad nicoise with tart lemonade. You'll catch yourself looking over your shoulder for the Eiffel Tower… or a panhandling homeless guy. $20

Sushi Groove South 1516 Folsom St. (11th St.) (415) 503-1950 Japanese. Follow your ears to the entrance, tucked between a parking lot and a salsa club. Nightly DJs keep house and downtempo thumping; sleek crowd, herded by Stepford Wife hostess, keeps it loud. Brightly lit sushi bar, dim tables in back where votive candles dot the walls. It's more about the scene than the sushi, but the cilantro roll easily carries the beat. Another Martel & Nabiel production. $35

Tu Lan 8 6th St. (Market St.) (415) 626-0927 Vietnamese. Amazing food in downright crappy location. Word-of-mouth dingy treasure. Inside: tiny, plain, filled with gritty locals. Delicate spring rolls, tender barbecue pork over crispy rice noodles. If you need atmosphere, get it to go. Or head upstairs to avoid Market Street crackheads and the sight of Raiders jersey–wearing chef sweating furiously over the wok. $15

Zuppa 564 Fourth St. (Bryant St.) (415) 777-5900 Italian. From the folks behind Globe, a place that knows how to party. Industrial hideaway packing in cool arty-farty types and off-duty chef pals feasting on chiffon-thin prosciutto and small plates of rustic fabulosities. Shiny red meat slicer imported from Italy is the original bad boy, so pay it some respect. Flirty staff, communal table, dinner-party vibe. Let the night begin. $35 ★ **BlackBook**

NIGHTLIFE SoMa & Potrero Hill

Anu 43 6th St. (Market & Mission Sts.) (415) 543-3505 Good music, better drinks, no cover. Sleazy street may be a downer, but this Irish-owned bar is like the Brady Bunch living room, except cooler. Funky orange lighting and love-bead curtain hiding the turntables. Pulsing UK house, cute European accents, young clubbers eyeing each other and tipping back mango vodkas while cutting up the new dance floor.

Arrow Bar 10 6th St. (Market St.) (415) 255-7920 Art deco smacks up against Cro-Magnon. Back widens into dusky cave with sparkling stalactites and flickering candles. Spot-on DJ every night playing anything from psych disco to indie rock. Thursdays and Saturdays post-mod shoegazers pack 'em in. If we only had a nickel for every Von Dutch brim. Late-night spot, so don't freak out if you show up at 11:30 and it's empty.

Bloom's Saloon 1318 18th St. (Missouri & Texas Sts.) (415) 552-6707 Old-fashioned saloon well stocked with rowdy, baseball-watching locals. Commitment to antiquity overwhelmed by Giants and 49ers banners and TVs broadcasting games. Huge beer selection. If you can't keep up with the fans, escape to the back patio.

Brain Wash Café and Laundromat 1122 Folsom St. (7th & 8th Sts.) (415) 861-3663 Raise your hand if you hate doing laundry. Thought so. What if you could drink while your clothes spun in the dryer? Laundromat/café combo is so the answer. Decent burgers and bar fare, variety of beverages. Live music or comedy almost every night. Grab an espresso and start folding, or chug some liquid courage and step up during open mic. Freaky locals will love you for it.

Butter 354 11th St. (Folsom & Harrison Sts.) (415) 863-5964 Total white trash, complete with tin roof and aluminum trailer kitchen serving Tater-tots, Ho-Hos and Swanson TV dinners. Bar opens onto street, making it feel like someone yanked up their garage door and started selling PBR from the keg. Funky art and Dukes of Hazzard projected onto walls. Former dot-com hotspot doesn't bring crowds like it used to, but still the best place around for a Jell-O shot.

Club Six 60 6th St. (Market & Mission Sts.) (415) 531-6593 Warehouse-style club is a crowd-pleaser. Promoters bringing in house legends and underground hip-hop. Ground floor like frat-house living room with circular couches snaking right down the middle, funky downtown crowd drinking from plastic cups. Hot, dark, low-ceilinged basement, reeking of stale beer.

Connecticut Yankee 100 Connecticut St. (17th St.) (415) 552-4440 Oh New England transplant feeling a bit homesick, this is the place for you. Plastered with Red Sox, Bruins and Celts paraphernalia, even Boston-themed sandwiches on the menu. A Bill Buckner, anyone? Act like a true Mass-hole and curse the Bambino (and A-Rod). Or just duck past red and white banners and check out the sunny back patio.

The EndUp 401 6th St. (Harrison St.) (415) 646-0999 Trannies, tweaky birds, diehard house heads cutting up the dance floor at this legendary after-hours. Around since the '70s, still going strong. Fake flame sconces and disco balls, pool tables and pinball, back patio garden with waterfall and deck. Deep and vocal house for anything-goes kinda crowd. The T-dance from 6 a.m. Sunday straight through Monday morning is still a laugh and perfect for people watching, just not nearly as gay as it once was. **BlackBook**

Hotel Utah 500 4th St. (Bryant St.) (415) 546-6300. Owners may have changed, but the look stays the same, just like your favorite shirt from the '70s. Bizarre knick-knacks covering the walls, balcony in back shaped like stern of old ship (where live bands play nightly). Fairly good bar food. Burgers, onion rings, 12 beers on tap. Eavesdrop on slurred geek speak from Wired editors in the corner.

Kelly's Mission Rock 817 China Basin (Mariposa St.) (415) 626-5355. Multi-level club on prime SF Bay real estate doubling as great lunch spot. Balcony over-looking the water is absolute perfection on a sunny day, especially when you factor in the calamari. At night, entire building threatens to collapse from crowd of B&Ts and Gen-Y ravers gyrating to electronic beats on four impromptu dance floors. Warmer months play host to legendarily scary Second Sunday parties.

Lit Lounge 101 6th St. (Mission St) (415) 278-0940. Part of new wave of low-cover bars along squalid 6th Street. Eclectic lounge adapts to your mood. Feeling mellow? Kick back in a velvet chair and eye the cute rocker chick sipping a 'tini. Looking for a beat? Step onto decent-sized dance floor to DJs mixing up J-Kwon and Duran Duran with everything in between. Owner Jennifer hustling behind bar to serve up Cuba-worthy mojitos and PBR on tap.

Mezzanine 444 Jessie St. (6th St.) (415) 625-8880 Circuit boys, rejoice! Saturday gay party for those mourning the loss of Club Townsend. Cheesy fast beats throbbing on Funktion One system as sweat flies off shirtless muscles straight into Sunday morning. Friday nights the straights hold court with Dutch trance and UK progressive house. Go on the odd cool-approved night thrown by Blasthaus. It's called a "gallery," but most nights the only thing adorning the wall are trainspotters.

Mighty 119 Utah St. (15th St.) (415) 626-7001 Another gallery-cum-dance club with bumpin' sound system and skilled DJs like Miguel Migs and crew on Saturdays. Exposed brick, massive wood columns, graffiti on the walls, bar from an old ice cream freezer. Wild Planet graphics on screen over main room.

111 Minna 111 Minna St. (2nd St.) (415) 974-1719 Also an art gallery, but no one's looking at the walls. Cheap cover ($5) and varied tunes bring in healthy does of posers. DJs from 5 to 10 p.m. make Wednesday night "Qool" a popular happy hour for fancy 20something professionals and past-their-prime ravers and burning man types.

The Stud 399 9th St. (Harrison St.) (415) 863-6623. Friendliest gay bar and dance floor in town. Pinball, yes; blue balls, no. Tuesday's the night for Trannyshack (10 years strong and counting). Saturdays mean Sugar, with house heads rolling and tweaking and bumping and grinding till 4 am. Drinks are cheap like 1989. Bathroom is like Trainspotting and over 25 years old. Be prepared.

Studio Z 314 11th (Folsom & Harrison Sts.) (415) 252-7666 Live something every night, though just as likely to be political rant as jazz band. Rough brick walls and high ceilings like being behind curtain of old theater. Art exhibits, reggae shows, rap contests, random DJs. If the bulky doorman has the nerve to suggest there's a cover, you can blag it fairly easily.

Ten15 Folsom 1015 Folsom St. (6th St.) (415) 431-1200 Hey dude, you got my glowstick? Twentysomething B&Ts, experimenting Asian cliques and various hoochies and tourists. Mulitilevel club with trance and UK progressive house (yawn) soundtrack. Various monthlies bring in the Burning Man set freaking to breakbeats and other odd sounds. Better hide that stash, because security here means business.

Thee Parkside 1600 17th St. (Wisconsin St.) (415) 503-0393 Rock venue. Band posters covering walls, Johnny Cash to Beatles to Sleepy Labeef on jukebox, bartenders channeling the drummer from the Strokes. Ample seating, room for dancing, decent burgers, wings and fries. Large patio with bar and ping-pong table.

Thirsty Bear Brewing Company 661 Howard St. (3rd St.) (415) 974-0905. Decent brewery. Lame crowd and location. Brewpub usually has nine of its own beers on tap, along with decent Spanish tapas. During the week, after-work revelers digging into fried calamari and potatoes with garlic aoli. Large open space filled with metal tanks do nothing for acoustics, so raise your voice along with your glass.

SOMA & POTRERO HILL

Wish 1539 Folsom St. (11th & 12th Sts.) (415) 278-9474 Dark curtains, votive candles, leather footstools, mellow vibe. After-work regulars enjoying $2 beers and free popcorn during late happy hour. Spillover from nearby clubs on weekends. After 8 p.m., DJs bounce typical SF house off cement walls.

XYZ 181 3rd St. (Howard St.) (415) 817-7836. Be in black with cell phone in hand as you part the silver-beaded curtain. Slice of LA, but then again what did you expect from the W? High-tech minimalist—neon bar changes color, menu for adjoining restaurant displayed on LCD screen in the window. Dave and Greg tossing back dirty martinis while pondering how the other half lives. Evening DJs, but is anyone listening?

_____

_____

_____

_____

_____

_____

_____

_____

_____

_____

_____

_____

"Leaving San Francisco is like saying goodbye to an old sweetheart.

You want to linger as long as possible. " —Walter Cronkite

MARINA & COW HOLLOW (map p. 122)

It's not just a neighborhood; it's an urban singleton's Pleasantville. Mention the **Marina** or **Cow Hollow** anywhere else in town, and you're guilty on every yuppie count. Blissfully unaware of what lies beyond their borders, the clique of blonde, blonder, blondest and their clean-cut pals call these two 'hoods home for good reason. Whether they're slumming it at the Gap, reading the Wall Street Journal at Starbucks, devouring a blistered pizza at **A16**, watching the game over brews at the **Final Final**, or hitting the Stairmaster at Gorilla Sports with the latest Us Weekly, locals have few reasons to leave this part of town (except to grab an ice blended at the Coffee Bean on the way to the crew's Tahoe pad). One needn't want for outdoor drinking spots, college deja-vu, or organized sports in this breeding ground for the blindingly white-toothed and the jauntily J. Crewed. Golden retrievers, baseball caps, black Jettas, REI gear all a plus. Drunken stumbling shambles down Lombard on a Saturday night practically required. So grab your favorite investment banker and meet us there. We'll be navigating each corner of **the notorious Marina Triangle**, swapping stock tips over sushi at **Ace Wasabi**, ordering it up Doggie Style at **Pizza Orgasmica**, and hiding out from the hordes in the darkness at **Brazen Head**. Oh, the glory of it all.

RESTAURANTS Marina & Cow Hollow

A16 2355 Chestnut St. (Scott and Divisadero Sts.) (415) 771-2216 Italian. Greenwich Village brick exterior, sophisticated interior plus vintage foosball table. Buzzing wine bar serving well-to-do neighborhood newlyweds out to prove they still know how to have fun with their friends. Excellent Southern Italian and California wine list, Neapolitan cuisine, simple blistered funghi pizza that will put you off Domino's for good. Just be prepared to wait for it. +$35 **BlackBook**

Ace Wasabi's Rock 'n' Roll Sushi 3339 Steiner St. (Chestnut and Lombard Sts.) (415) 567-4903 Japanese. Marina sushi hotspot where every hour is happy hour. Meet Alex P. Keaton and his friends after work. Scope out crowd over Sapporos up front, schmooze with chefs at the sushi bar, or dine in peace in the back room. Always busy but surprisingly short wait. Harmless yummy yuppie fun. +$20

Alegrias Food From Spain 2018 Lombard St. (Webster and Fillmore Sts.) (415) 929-8888 Spanish. Slice of Spain on anything-but-scenic Lombard. Crisp white walls, mounted ceramic plates, flamenco shawls thrown over wooden screens. Small plates since before they were trendy. Espinacas a la Catalana means sautéed spinach with garlic, raisins, apples, and pinenuts, plus bonus points with your date for pronunciation. Muy bueno, señorita. $30

Baker Street Bistro 2953 Baker St. (Filbert and Greenwich Sts.) (415) 931-1475 French. Escargots, croque monsieur, crème caramel. So far, so French. BYOB (with corkage fee) or drink theirs. Blissful brunch or decadent dinner. Perfect for your "I know this great little French place" collection. Accent of waitress confirms your suspicion—this place is legit. Airy interior, outdoor seating. Bistro fare with garden flair. $30

Betelnut Pejiu Wu 2030 Union St. (Buchanan and Webster Sts.) (415) 929-8855 Pan-Asian. Getting a table feels like getting through customs. Linger at straight-outta-Shanghai bar and trade conspiracy theories with fellow diners about estimated wait time. Red lacquer and more action than a Bruce Lee film on display in open kitchen. Glazed pork short ribs, claypot curried fish, awkward first dates all around providing endless entertainment. $35

Bistro Aix 3340 Steiner St. (Lombard and Chestnut Sts.) (415) 202-0100 New American. Foodies flock to old reliable. Brasserie feel with dark woods, black-and-whites on the wall. Petition for a cozier ambiance on the patio, where heat lamps combat the San Francisco chill. 23 wines by the glass, 80 by the bottle, and chef Jonathan Beard serving up favorites in fresh calamari, ahi tuna, and lamb. Ace in the hole. $25

Brazen Head 3166 Buchanan St. (Greenwich St.) (415) 921-7600 Traditional American. Exceptional late-night dining with Sherlock Holmes décor. Diamond in the (not so) rough hood, named for oldest pub in Ireland, with cult of Brazen Burger lovers swearing theirs is the best red meat in town. Lack of sign and framed portraits of rakes, poets, and royals make for gentlemen's-club ambiance. Locals crowd in come the wee hours for Bond-worthy martinis from über-bartender Jimmy, plus full dinner menu till 1 a.m. $30 **BlackBook**

Greens Fort Mason, Bldg. A (415) 771-6222 Vegetarian. Who knew a no-meat restaurant could be so pricey? Old waterfront warehouse turned dining destination since 1979. Unbeatable bay views, inventive veggie creations, mix of tourists and grown-up/dressed-up hippies. Think Dharma with a hint of Greg. Vegan options, too. $35

The Grove 2250 Chestnut St. (Avila St.) (415) 474-4843 American. Central Perk goes rustic. Gang's all here—and they brought their laptops. Sit outside and savor stellar Arnold Palmers. Overpay for order-at-the-counter gourmet offerings and utopian Sunday ambiance. Granola served with strawberries and bananas, tuna fish sandwich, Beat poet coffeehouse–sized cappuccinos. Perfect for solo mission or meeting up with friends. $13

Home on Union 2032 Union St. (Buchanan St.) (415) 931-5006 Comfort Food. Spinoff of popular Castro original, though one glance round the dining room should alert you to change in crowd. Slight bump up in prices, too. Pot roast and sloppy Joes make repeat appearance, co-starring banana bread pudding with bourbon sauce. Bring the stomach pump. -$30 ★

Isa 3324 Steiner St. (Chestnut & Lombard Sts.) (415) 567-9588 French. Francophile small plates on twinkling fairytale tented back patio. Groups of cultured 30-somethings staging pseudo-dinner parties. Steeped in too-good-to-be-true ambiance. Baked goat cheese with tomatoes and pine nuts, mussels, tender flat-iron steak with tarragon mustard, eclectic wine list. Isn't life grand? +$30

La Canasta 3006 Buchanan St. (Union & Filbert Sts.) (415) 474-2627 Mexican. Local sweethearts in sweatpants satisfy hangover hankerings. Clean, fresh, authentic Mexican in its truest form: takeaway homemade tamales, grande burritos, taquitos rancheros. Sit outside and monopolize the one bench that serves as their sitting area. Smirk at health nuts refueling at neighboring Jamba Juice. $8

La Table O&Co. 3352 Steiner St. (Chestnut and Lombard Sts.) (415) 440-9040 Mediterranean. Pan-Mediterranean bistro-cum-olive-oil boutique done up in charming provincial décor. Like dining in French version of Williams-Sonoma: Try it, then buy it. Warm goat cheese terrine, frisee salad, rabbit rillette. Upscale farmers-market devotees sip wine and sample olive oils from sidewalk tables. C'est si bon. -$22

Left at Albuquerque 2140 Union St. (Fillmore and Webster Sts.) (415) 749-6700 Tex-Mex. Disneyfied roadhouse decor with matching ambiance. Listen closely and you'll hear the ties loosening come happy hour. Scrumptious tortilla chips and more than 50 tequilas on offer, but skip the house brand unless you're driving. See table next to you for reason behind "limit one per customer" 66-oz. margarita rule. Overpriced guacamole, bargain-price blackened fish tacos.. $22

Liverpool Lil's 2942 Lyon St. (Lombard and Greenwich Sts.) (415) 921-6664 Pub fare. Old-world feel with neighborhood crew. Plan the American Revolution over fish and chips and top-of-the-line cheeseburgers in dark, woodsy headquarters oppo-site picturesque Presidio Gate. Beer garden with outdoor tables and historic sports memorabilia. Dressed-down locals nurse Sunday-night blues. Dinner til top of the mornin'. $20

Luisa's 1851 Union St. (Laguna and Octavia Sts.) (415) 563-4043 Italian. North Beach–caliber Italian that somehow got separated from the flock. Homemade pasta, veal and lamb chops, possibly the best gnocchi in town, wine bottles hanging from the ceiling. Sopranos-suitable Luisa greets you at the door and shows you photos from her Sophia Loren–ingénue days. $25

Lux 2263 Chestnut St. (Pierce and Scott Sts.) (415) 567-2998 Asian Fusion. There's low-light ambiance, and then there's no-light darkness. Tight-squeeze tables make for a game of food Tetris with your plates. Zinc-topped bar, crimson walls, Bebe poncho–wearing clientele. Menu identity crisis: Truffle cheese fondue with grilled country bread and duck confit and pancetta egg rolls. From the people who brought you around-the-corner Isa. $35

Mas Sake 2030 Lombard St. (Fillmore and Webster Sts.) (415) 440-1505 Japanese. A Japanese restaurant with a Spanish word in its name? You were asking for it. Actress/model waitresses imported from L.A. serve up overpriced family-style sushi for 24th-birthday parties. Sake bombing is order of the night. Motto reads "Mad Sushi, Mad Beats, Fresh Flavor, Fresh Skin." Don't say we didn't warn you. $26

Pizza Orgasmica 3157 Fillmore St. (Greenwich and Filbert Sts.) (415) 931-5300 Italian. Leave the bar, do not pass go, do not collect $200, proceed directly here. Smell the seduction for miles. Adam and Eve painting on the wall, not that you'd remember. Late-night pizza joint morphs into last-chance meat market. Pies named Ménage a Trois, Doggie Style, and Ecstasy, also available by the slice. Better than you-know-what. $10

PlumpJack Café 3127 Fillmore St. (Filbert and Greenwich Sts.) (415) 563-4755 New American. Part of empire that Gavin Newsom built. Located next door to debauchery, with upscale, approachable atmosphere. Superb beet salad with goat cheese, chocolate devil's food cake that could launch a thousand ships. Food done well, in take-your-visiting-parents kind of way. Flawless wine list with no markup, be-our-guest service. Cozy. $50

Pluto's 3258 Scott St. (Chestnut and Lombard Sts.) (415) 775-8867 California Cuisine. How you imagine Mom would cook if she did Thanksgiving all year round. Carved turkey, stuffing, grilled mushrooms, rosemary focaccia, all for order at the counter at ridiculously cheap prices. Steer clear after Gorilla Sports yoga class, when annoyingly centered post-workout types make a beeline for the blue-ribbon salad bar. $10

Rica 1838 Union St. (Laguna and Octavia Sts.) (415) 474-3773. Nouveau Spanish. Taco lounge where Euro-clubbing royalty mix with Sex and the City extras, courtesy of nightlife kings Martel and Nabiel. Guacamole made to order, perfectly greasy tortilla chips, holy moley–worthy mole chicken. Early-evening Stan Getz on the stereo, minimalist décor with a big-night-out feel. Excuse me, your Prada is in my empanada. Packs them in. The pre-party is here.

Rose's Café 2298 Union St. (Steiner St.) (415) 775-2200 Cal-Italian. Daytime destination for ladies who lunch or push strollers, plus couples out for refined weekend booze-up. Anyone who's anyone snags an outdoor table. Brunch that's heavy on the presentation, house-specialty thin pizzas. Relax, stay awhile. Good-morning-sunshine interior. $25

Yoshida-Ya 2909 Webster St. (Union and Filbert Sts.) (415) 346-3431 Japanese. No shoes, good service. Ditch Western ways and sit barefoot at traditional low tables with recessed well seating. Keep it casual at the sushi bar downstairs. No wait even on the weekends. Seasonal assorted sashimi, traditional sushi menu, selection of hot and cold sake to go with. Teriyaki entrees for the timid. Mmmm… Zen. $25

NIGHTLIFE Marina & Cow Hollow

Balboa Café 3199 Fillmore St. (Greenwich St.) 415-921-3944 Buckingham Palace for SF royalty. Gavin Newsom's pet project (aside from the city itself, that is). Power politicos talk urban planning over Maker's Mark at the corner table, while finance types and gold-diggers clink glasses of PlumpJack wine at the mahogany bar. Live the high life, or just pretend you do.

Bar None 1980 Union St. (Buchanan and Laguna Sts.) (415) 409-4469 Ever wonder where UC college grads go to mourn the loss of their PlayStation-tournaments days? The Abercrombie & Fitch frat party resumes every weekend at this subterranean venue. Escape the sticky floors and take your drink to the heated patio, where a drunken crying girl chain-smokes and sobs as her friends tell her why he's not worth it.

Bluelight 1979 Union St. (Buchanan and Laguna Sts.) (415) 922-5510 Not just a clever name. Full of '90s décor, from the tracklit mirror behind the bar down to the glowing electric-blue light fixtures. Taco Tuesdays mean $1 tacos, $2 Coronas, $3 margaritas and a clamoring crowd. Singles scene for yuppies-in-training. Kinda nice, in a notch-above-Olive-Garden kind of way. Retractable roof in the back means on weekends you can have your sunshine and play pool too.

Bus Stop 1901 Union St. (Buchanan and Laguna Sts.) (415) 567-6905 "Sometimes you want to go, where everybody…" looks the same. Will Hunting and his East Coast–transplant buddies don white baseball caps and cheer for their alma mater. PGA Tour Championship in the back and brews with the boys—lots of boys. How 'bout them apples?

City Tavern 3200 Fillmore St. (Lombard and Greenwich Sts.) (415) 567-0918 The most relaxed of the so-called "triangle bars" (Eastside West and Balboa Café being the other two corners), with come-as-you-are vibe, people-watching windows, and reasonably priced drinks. Civilized sports bar, aside from the occasional Sloppy Joe and his belligerent girlfriend—they should have been cut off a few rounds back.

Cozmo's Corner Grill 2001 Chestnut St. (Fillmore St.) (415) 351-0175 Casually upscale meat market where after-work suits swill and stalk their prey. Brick walls, banquettes, and desirable second-floor mezzanine. More cell phones then you can shake a stick at. Three-star review from infamously hard-to-please SF Chronicle food critic Michael Bauer overshadowed by oppressive singles scene. Fresh-baked chocolate-chip cookies that would make Mrs. Fields cry.

Delaney's 2241 Chestnut St. (Pierce and Scott Sts.) (415) 931-8529 Cheery Irish spot where someone's always at the bar. The final course of your Marina pub crawl with a late-night jukebox-fueled dance party for dessert. Alcoholics keep the place in business during the day and pass the baton to local yuppies at night. Under-the-radar private patio available for parties.

Donahue's Marina Lounge 2138 Chestnut St. (Steiner and Pierce Sts.) (415) 922-1475 Don't be fooled by the cartoonish "Hark! Cocktails!" sign out front—this watering hole-in-the-wall has a no-nonsense vibe about it. Gruff bartenders serve blue-collar boys on barstools who act like they own the place. Homer Simpson and his buddies meet up to drown their after-work/out-of-work sorrows and commiserate about the little woman.

Eastside West 3154 Fillmore St. (Greenwich and Filbert Sts.) (415) 885-4000 Supper club goes seafood. Come for the happy-hour oysters, stay for the booze. Monthly live jazz and a consistently laid-back Marina crowd. Sidewalk tables are prime real estate on weekends, when Gucci sunglasses–clad chicks accessorize their tracksuits with Louis Vuitton purses and sip too-sweet mojitos.

Final Final 2990 Baker St. (Greenwich and Lombard Sts.) (415) 931-7800 Sports bar dating back to Prohibition. Cavalcade of pub grub, from pizza cooked in a stone oven to hot dogs to popcorn. Smells like it, too. Ask to see the Elvis snifter from the owner's porcelain-snifter collection. Watch the game during the day alongside old-schoolers of the golf cap and cane variety. The younger sporty set stops by and stays the night.

Gravity 3251 Scott St. (Chestnut and Lombard Sts.) (415) 776-1928 Hey, it's Night at the Roxbury! Check in and get checked out. Oversized crimson and gold brushed-metal fireplace, in-demand banquettes, classic films on flat screens. MTV's The Grind on the dance floor, Jay-Z on the speakers, shorter line in the back-room bar. Spring break lives on.

HiFi 2125 Lombard St. (Fillmore and Steiner Sts.) (415) 345-8663 Look for the crowd of after-midnight overdone-its huddled on the sidewalk. Era-blending décor with a retro bent: Mondrian-styled stained-glass mural (check), disco ball (got it), vinyl studded bar (yup). Oversized back booth accommodates the dancing queen plus her rap video–sized entourage. Mixed crowd of hipper-than-usuals for the area, plus some sketchballs of the purse-snatching variety.

Horseshoe Tavern 2024 Chestnut St. (Fillmore and Steiner Sts.) (415) 346-1430 Preppy-athletic locals who live down the street pack in to watch the basket-/foot-/baseball game. Open since 1934, with the sepia-toned SF cityscape photos to prove it. Classic rock on the jukebox and owner Stefan Wever's snapshots on display. Giant horseshoe pièce de résistance mounted on the mirror in back.

La Barca 2036 Lombard St. (Webster and Fillmore Sts.) (415) 921-2221 Just as many flavors of worm juice as Baskin-Robbins has ice cream. Incidentally, it's a Mexican restaurant too—but everyone drinks their dinner. Stiff margs, stiffer competition for a bartender's attention. It's no neighborhood secret, as you'll see when Brian from Dublin leans on the wrought iron that looks shipped in from Universal Studios and asks if you know any other bars in the area.

MatrixFillmore 3138 Fillmore St. (Greenwich and Filbert Sts.) (415) 563-4180 Weekend warriors unite! Restored 1960s birthplace of Jefferson Airplane with a futuristic fireplace, plasma screen, floor-to-ceiling windows and sleek plum ottomans with serious lounge appeal. Cool, right? Wrong. The cheesy clientele put the trix in Matrix. On the bright side, there's never a cover, there's always a DJ, and the bartender mixes a mean spiced-tea mojito to help numb the pain.

Mauna Loa Club 3009 Fillmore St. (Union St.) (415) 563-5137 Aloha! Nothing Hawaiian here, except a feeling of escape. The only place on the block where not everyone's looking to get lei'ed. Wooden reproduction of Toulouse-Lautrec print carved by a friend of the original owners (who do indeed hail from the Big Island). Financial-analyst buddies mix with construction workers and aging sorority girls.

Nectar Wine Lounge 3330 Steiner St. (Chestnut and Lombard Sts.) (415) 345-1377 Sleek wine haven with make-a-night-of-it magic. Scene looks lifted from the cover of an ambient Late Night Lounge compilation, and sounds like it too. Ritzy clientele, scarlet back wall and an orchid on the bar positioned just so. Take the menu up on its pairing suggestions. **BlackBook**

Silver Clouds 1994 Lombard St. (Webster St.) (415) 922-1977 Karaoke hotspot attracting the usual suspects. Drama geeks who never made it arrive before 10 p.m. to secure their place on the song list, while the rest of the crowd (drunken folks en route from Mas Sake and La Barca) files in late in the evening for a laugh. Take a trip down Tom Jones and Rick Springfield lane. "It's not unusual" to be spilled on. Unbearably tolerant crowd encourages performances so terrible they're almost good—almost.

The Black Horse London Pub 1514 Union St. (Van Ness Ave. and Franklin St.) (415) 928-2414 Pull up a barstool with a few of your pals, and the place is instantly at capacity. Tiny hole-in-the-wall pub that sets Anglophile hearts afire. 30-something dressed-down locals on a first-name basis with the bartender, who serves cask-conditioned ale from Gilroy you can't get anywhere else in town. Proximity means you better get friendly with your neighbor at the bar, seeing as how you're sitting on his lap. In authentic pub fashion, it closes at 11 pm.

Tongue & Groove 2513 Van Ness Ave. (Union St.) (415) 928-0404 Eighties cover bands converge to play to their enraptured cult followings. Multitude of missed-the-'80s-the-first-time fans. Wear nothing and head to the back mezzanine to combat the heat of the tightly packed 200-person capacity venue. Hot fun in the summertime, all year round. Keep in mind, your nearest exit may be behind you.

"You know what it is? San Francisco is a golden handcuff with the key thrown away."

—John Steinbeck

PACIFIC HEIGHTS
& PRESIDIO HEIGHTS (map p. 123-125)

Clipped hedges, maids in uniform, and chauffeured Bentleys say it all. Just in case you were wondering how the other half lives, **Pac Heights** is here to show you. Not much folk out on the sidewalks, unless you count the dogwalker with the poodle or the gardener trimming topiaries; all the action takes place inside the turrets and castles belonging to clans with last names like Getty. Here we've got the Spreckels Mansion, home to Danielle Steel and her fashionista brood rocking their Proenza Schouler and Chanel couture. There we've got the usual private-school brats cutting calculus and brown-bagging it on the Lyon Street Steps. Upper Fillmore is the boutique strip, drawing tank-topped yoga hotties to the sundeck at International Orange and blueblood playboys in crested blazers swirling their Pernods at **Florio**. Further west in **Presidio Heights**, the estates get even bigger, the trust funds more bloated. Tour Seacliff for a peep at Robin Williams' puffy monstrosity, as well as the 7BDRM humdinger Sharon Stone once shared with mustachioed newspaperman Phil Bronstein. As for the 1,500-acre Presidio playground, with its fog-laced forests and coastal bluffs, even George Lucas and his ILM geeks couldn't ruin the picture. On a fine day, bring a picnic to Baker Beach and drink in the luscious Golden Gate views. (Just don't wander too far down unless you like your sandwich with a side of naked gay butt.) Catch us licking our chops at **Chez Nous**, doing ceviche three ways at **Fresca**, swimming in over our heads at the **Fish Bowl**, and going out with a roar at the **Lion's Den**.

RESTAURANTS Pacific Heights
& Presidio Heights

Cafe Lo Cubano 3401 California St. (Laurel St.) (415) 831-4672 Cuban Café. Pilates housewives park sport-utility strollers for chance to pick at overpriced empanadas and hot pressed sandwiches in Eames-knockoff interior. Dusk brings neighborhood hepcats and flirty USF coeds digging free Internet access over cafecitos. No Café Habana, but it'll do. Laurel Heights Social Club, indeed. -$18 ★

Chez Nous 1911 Fillmore St. (Bush St.) (415) 441-8044 Mediterranean. Gone in 60 seconds. Plates so small they belong in Gulliver's Travels. Irrepressible Gallic baker-turned-businessman Pascal Rigo behind scrumptious morsels of French-Med cuisine. Luscious lamb chops, herb-dusted pommes frites, warm apple crisp in Cote d'Azur atmosphere. Get here early or plan on cooling your heels. +$25

Desiree Café 39 Mesa St., Ste. 108 (Presidio Blvd.) (415) 561-2336 Californian. Tiny lunch cantina for San Francisco Film Centre. Former military barracks housing Presidio gourmet secret. Menu repeating ubiquitous farmers' market mantra, but why quibble when it clearly works? Breakfast, lunch, boxed picnics, weekly menus. My egg runneth over. $10

Elite Café 2049 Fillmore St. (California St.) (415) 346-8668 Cajun. The Big Easy does Fillmore, since 1981. Old bookie joint with some original cred still intact. Nice long bar to slurp oysters, read Esquire, or watch the game with the sound off. Deep mahogany booths, laissez-les-bons-temps-rouler attitude. Boisterous. $35 **BlackBook**

Eliza's 2877 California St. (Divisadero St.) (415) 621-4819 Chinese. Do believe the hype. Consistency and quality come with fresh ingredients prepared well. Iron Chef–worthy classics like crab rangoon and sesame chicken, plus imaginative mango beef or salmon with black bean sauce. No grease, good eats. $20

Ella's 500 Presidio Ave. (California St.) (415) 441-5669 American. Hurry up and wait! Fanatical citywide breakfast obsession, namely crisped chicken hash (see also fresh-baked sticky buns and chicken potpie). Stroller Nazis, sleepy couples, the fleece set, all toeing the line before 8 a.m. for chance to grub inside peach-walled haven. Come on, people. It's good, but is it that good? The word lemming comes to mind. $15

Florio 1915 Fillmore St. (Pine St.) (415) 775-4300 Brasserie. Solid neighborhood spot with aspirations of grandeur. Handsome, golden, and aglow with polished woods and Pac Heights gilded youth. Old money with subtle accents, as in cashmere crewnecks with Joe's Jeans and Hermès loafers. Tarragon-fueled béarnaise good enough to drink. Digestif of choice: Scotch on the rocks. $30

Fresca 2114 Fillmore St. (California St.) (415) 447-2668 Peruvian. Horrendous tribal-mask sign, tremendous Peruvian fare. Halibut ceviche, skillet-roasted rainbow trout, not-sure-it-fits-but-sure-glad-it's-there sangria. Open-air kitchen adds touch of theater, and front-row seats are yours at up-close-and-personal counter area. Vegetarians, beware. $25 **BlackBook**

Galette 2043 Fillmore St. (California St.) (415) 928-1300 Crepes. Breton-style organic buckwheat crepes from folks behind Chez Nous, so you know it's French. Authentically Gallic waitstaff with the vowels to prove it. Dry-to-the-bone cider sets off seafood crepe flambéed with Calvados. Simplicity is best. $22

Garibaldis 347 Presidio Ave. (Sacramento St.) (415) 563-8841 Cal-Med. Solid neighborhood favorite for upper-crust scions and aging junior socialites. Burberry headbands, Tod's driving mocs, Lacoste polos all a go. Seared day boat scallops (yawn), ahi tuna tartare (snooze), pan-roasted duck breast… Another mandarin martini, please. $40

Godzilla Sushi 1800 Divisadero St. (Bush St.) (415) 931-1773 Japanese. Simple sushi on the cheap, sans giant lizard–induced Tokyo wreckage. Young Kirin-swilling crowd, chaos-managing staff, roll-you-out-the-door portions. Don't count on best sashimi ever. Do count on Japanese feast at a fair tariff. $20

Jackson Fillmore 2506 Fillmore St. (Jackson St.) (415) 346-5288 Italian. Cozy, minimalist red-sauce mecca with mean seafood fra diavolo. Bare-bones décor that you pay for, in that paper-placemats-and-counter-seating/high-prices kind of way. It's loud, it's cramped. It's carbs to the max. You can't get enough. For dessert: espresso-soaked affogato. $30

La Méditerranée 2210 Fillmore St. (Sacramento St.) (415) 921-2956 Middle Eastern. Tops a Laugh In miniskirt–sized list of best dinner deals in town. Greatest hits: Middle Eastern plate, tender chicken pomegranate, blond Lillet over ice. Skip tomato bisque, known outside Greece as marinara sauce. East Village bohemian beauties serving up practically-giving-it-away grub. At these prices, the locals are suspicious. $20

Leticia's 2301 Fillmore St. (Clay St.) (415) 922-1722 Mexican. Taquitos and other typical Chicano fare in the midst of gringoville. Shouldn't surprise you that this is no Mission District gem. Overpriced entrees, weak drinks, sluggish service making for wish-we-could-turn-back-time dining experience. But if you're craving Mexican, what you gonna do? $12

Osaka Japanese Restaurant 1923 Fillmore St. (Pine St.) (415) 346-6788 Japanese. Is the Green River Roll an homage to Creedence? Eh, who cares. All the usual sushi suspects, plus some creative new combos (Vegitalian: cucumber, sprouts, gobo root, mint leaf!?). No atmosphere to speak of, it's just you and your hamachi. $30

Quince 1701 Octavia St. (Bush St.) (415) 775-8500 Italian. Fancy-pants darling of the food critics, with grandparents-dining-room décor. Diff'rent Strokes dad–looka-like crowd, wedding-of-the-year fare. Inspired Italian cooking from chef Michael Tusk. Because when else will you eat nettles? Seasonality-sensitive menu changes frequently. Excellent wine list. $50

Sociale 3665 Sacramento St. (Spruce St.) (415) 921-3200 Italian. When the moon hits your eye like a plate of fried olives, that's Sociale. Cinematic courtyard (heated, even), golden-hued dining room, hearty country fare. Tender braised short ribs atop perfect polenta. Servers playing matchmaker for J. Crew catalog rejects. When the world seems to shine like you've had too much wine, it's time for dessert: sfingi, honey-glazed doughnuts with too-good-to-be-true milkshake. $40

Via Veneto 2244 Fillmore St. (Sacramento St.) (415) 346-9211 Italian. Attractive flower-box façade, decent and inexpensive pasta spot. Don't expect too much, and you'll be just fine. Ample servings, bright and airy atmosphere, rusty service. Inoffensive and forgettable. $20

Vivande Porta Via 2125 Fillmore St. (Sacramento St.) (415) 346-4430 Italian. Fully functional trattoria inside fully functional Italian grocery. Owner Carlo Middione, cookbook author and TV chef, turning out housemade sausage, mushroom pâté, asparagus wrapped in prosciutto with shaved reggiano to eat in or take away. Real Modena balsamic vinegar starting at $75 for 100 ml, just in case you forgot which neighborhood you were in. $25

NIGHTLIFE Pacific Heights & Presidio Heights

Fish Bowl Bar & Grill 1854 Divisadero St. (Pine St.) (415) 775-3630 Playboy owner keeps hometown party going. Lively dive festooned with surfboards, mermaids, abalone shells with Pepperidge Farm goldfish. Eminem to Lynyrd Skynyrd on the jukebox. Bad-girl socialites dancing on the bar Hilton-style, guest bartenders on Wednesday nights. Deep-sea fishbowl drinks with four straws to share. **BlackBook**

Frankie's Bohemian Café 1862 Divisadero St. (Pine St.) (415) 921-4725 Prague on the Pacific, and stop number two on Divisadero pub crawl. Czech-American spot with deep red walls and bottomless 22-ounce beers. You best believe those extra six ounces catch up with you, and quick! But then again, they did say this place was bohemian.

G Bar 488 Presidio Ave. (California St.) (415) 409-4227 Like a mini-W Hotel in Presidio Heights. Small and stylish in-house bar of Laurel Inn, with slight '60s twinge. Used to be hot, now just chill, which is kind of better anyway. Blue blazers and bluebloods, techie travelers and cute chicks in pairs. Nice for the 'hood.

Harry's Bar 2020 Fillmore St. (Pine St.) (415) 921-1000 Polished neighborhood drinking hole stocking ambiguously titled businessmen who use "product" and go through 10 business cards a night. Mahogany bar, mirrored walls, cozy local vibe. Six bucks for a Niman Ranch burger and fries is a helluva deal.

Lion Pub 2062 Divisadero St. (Sacramento St.) (415) 567-6565 Inexplicably referred to as the Lion's Den, though there's no sign, and that's not its name. Allegedly bit of a ____ den, as well. Pac Heights preppies, aging Castro queens, fresh-squeezed juices from orange to cantaloupe making for unbeatable blended drinks. Free cheese and crackers, not that anyone's eating. **BlackBook**

Solstice 2801 California St. (Divisadero St.) (415) 359-1222 Lounge with decent restaurant attached, almost as afterthought. Sunken area with purple orb-shaped ottomans and velvet banquettes playing host to chick-heavy singles scene, of the halter-top-and-raspberry-mojito variety. Good enough.

_____

_____

_____

_____

_____

_____

_____

_____

_____

_____

_____

"One day if I do go to heaven...I'll look around and say, 'It ain't bad, but it ain't San Francisco. "

—Herb Caen

HAYES VALLEY & CIVIC CENTER

(map p.127)

Behold gentrification at its finest. Powell's Soul Food has sadly departed (in search of more reasonable rent in the Western Addition), and now **Hayes Valley's** reinvention as bourgeois boutique heaven is complete. From M.A.C.'s high-end la moda, baby, to baby moda at Lavish and baby designers renting their own racks at RAG, this is SF's own little Nolita-in-training, a temple to unnecessary consumption. It wasn't always like this, of course: Back before the Loma Prieta quake of '89, the Central Freeway loomed over the 'hood like an evil obelisk, harboring many a crack deal in its shadow. There's still that die-hard contingent who claim they liked it better that way and have the battle scars to prove it, but the rest of us consider it a fair trade. Look close and you'll spot a couple of cool patios lurking undercover: the back garden at **Frjtz** (skip the salads, double up on crepes) and the sunny courtyard at **Arlequin** (our venue of choice for a gourmet BLT). Nearby **Civic Center**, whose monuments kinda look like Paris if you squint, is mostly an outpost for City Hall slaves or rich folks heading to the opera or symphony. You'll find blue-hairs mingling with the suits over Mai Tais at **Trader Vic's**, or prancing tipsy from pre-curtain frolickings at **Jardiniere**. Us, we've found our circuit, and we're sticking to it. It's about the schnitzel at **Suppenkuche**, the matzo balls at **Moishe's**, the heavy petting at **Hôtel Biron**, and the zinc-topped bar at **Zuni**, which never fails to make us fall in love with SF all over again.

RESTAURANTS Hayes Valley & Civic Center

Absinthe 398 Hayes St. (Gough St.) (415) 551-1590 Bistro. Fin de siècle dining in Moulin Rouge setting. Oysters, lavender crème brulée, and blood-orange cocktails, though no actual absinthe or Nicole Kidman last time we checked. Slightly snooty waitstaff and pretty pricey drinks, but who cares when the warm polenta with marscarpone is so good? Some sidewalk tables, some homeless folks, so sit at your own discretion. $40

Arlequin 384 Hayes St. (Gough St.) (415) 626-1211 French. Absinthe's baby sister isn't your ordinary sliver of a sandwich shop. Croque Arlequin, prosciutto and brie, albacore tuna with coriander vinaigrette, best housemade potato chips ever. Darling community garden out back full of lithe, spaghetti-strapped shopgirls. Ahhh. -$15 **BlackBook**

Ananda Fuara 1298 Market St. (Larkin St.) (415) 621-1994 Vegetarian. Not much from the outside. Inside, serenity now for vegetarians on the cheap. Adventurous neatloaf sandwich, plus more innocuous veggie burgers and such. Run by students of spiritual teacher and poet Sri Chinmoy. What, you never heard of him?! -$15

Bistro Clovis 1596 Market St. (Franklin St.) (415) 864-0231 French Bistro. Proudly putting on the moves for almost 20 years. Quiet enough for your murmured sweet nothings. Tuck into cassoulet or boeuf bourguignonne, order the three-glass wine flight, and don't pass on the tarte Tatin. Lace curtains, lots of mirrors, classic bistro feel. +$30

Canto Do Brasil 41 Franklin St. (Oak & Page Sts.) (415) 626-8727 Brazilian. Who needs Carnaval? Pulsing Afro-Caribbean beats, vibrant blue accents, lush tropical plants, and you, dancing a samba on the beaches of Rio. A few caipirinhas and a bite of feijoada, and you'll be shaking it like Charo. $25

Citizen Cake 399 Grove St. (Gough St.) (415) 861-2228 American. Delectable savories, like tuna sandwich with cornichons, pecans, and apples, or spinach salad with lardons and poached egg. But who are they kidding, it's all about those desserts. Worship at the altar of pastry goddess Elizabeth Falkner for her Purple Rain or Peach Pain Perdu. $30

Culinary Academy's Carême Room Restaurant 625 Polk St. (Turk St.) (415) 216-4329 Varied. Even Rocco had to start somewhere. Dine on creations of wannabe chefs in cavernous, antiseptic dining room. So the ambiance is kinda like a Vegas buffet, and the dishes are inconsistent. But hey, it's cheaper than you'd get elsewhere, and you're helping the rookie effort. $20

Espetus 1686 Market St. (415) 552-8792 Brazilian. A vegetarian's worst nightmare. But for some, nothing says dinnertime like meat on a stick. Gauchos roam churrascaria with skewers of beef, pork, chicken, or lamb, then slice it up tableside. Roam, slice, roam, slice. Atkins-friendly, but you know when to say when. Don't you? $40

Flipper's 482 Hayes St. (Gough & Octavia Sts.) (415) 552-8880 American. Burger purists beware. International concoctions like the Copenhagen Way (blue cheese, walnuts, beets) hang out with the likes of the Flipper Dipper (teriyaki). So-so service, diverse clientele (gender-benders from Marlena's next door), fab patio for soaking up those rare SF rays. $10

Frjtz 579 Hayes St. (Laguna St.) (415) 864-7654 Belgian. Recipe for a perfect Sunday afternoon: one order of Belgian fries, one savory crepe, Chimay on tap, and a spot on the back patio with a book or buddy. DJ Frjtz on Fridays wears his sunglasses at night. Once Mad Magda's Russian Tea Room, back in the day. $15

Hayes Street Grill 320 Hayes St. (Franklin St.) (415) 863-5545 Seafood. This joint started the 'hood. On the street since 1979, it's old-school S.F.—not as cool as Tadich Grill, but it'll do. Co-owned by local foodie/writer Patricia Unterman. Fresh fish done up traditional, served to guys and dolls with names like Frankie and Lois. Take grandma for her birthday. +$35

Il Borgo 500 Fell St. (Laguna St.) (415) 255-9108 Italian. Why wrestle with North Beach parking demons when there's this Hayes Valley gem? Pulls out all the stops: checkered tablecloths, Chianti bottles with candles, Italian murals. Pillowy home-made bread and pizzas, plus tasty ravioli and gnocchi. Paging Lady, Tramp, and that strand of spaghetti. $25

Indigo 687 McAllister St. (Franklin & Gough Sts.) (415) 673-9353 New American. Mix of Hayes Valley slackers, culturists before curtain call, and suits from City Hall. Indigo hues abound, no surprise, giving the place a lunar appeal. Sister restaurant to trendy Jade Bar around the corner. $49 prix-fixe buys you starter, entree, dessert, and free-flowing wine to match. +$35

J's Pots of Soul 203 Octavia St. (Page St.) (415) 861-3230 Soul Food/Breakfast. Hangover central. Face-plant into a greasy pork chop or stack of pancakes with clarified butter, then wash it all down with booze-sopping grits. Divey but sweet little diner off the beaten track. Friendly staff with pots of soul to spare. $10

Jardiniere 300 Grove St. (Franklin St.) (415) 861-5555 French. Truly elegant set-ting, truly dazzling food. Dust off the Armani and practice those table manners. Oh, and plan on dropping a paycheck. It's fun eating like old money every now and then, especially in surroundings like a giant champagne flute. +$50

Moishe's Pippic 425 Hayes St. (Gough St.) (415) 431-2440 Jewish Deli. Only place in SF you can find matzo ball soup like Bubbelah used to make. Crunchy, salty dills, chopped liver, hot brisket on Friday, latkes and applesauce, and hot pas-trami on rye done up Chicago-style, plus Moishe behind the counter not taking any shit. Enough to make a Catholic girl convert. $15

Paul K 199 Gough St. (Oak St.) (415) 552-7132 Mediterranean. Sleek and sexy little devil, with one part opera, one part edgy crowd. Pomegranate Martini is a must. Exotic ingredients like harissa, sumac, and medjool dates in sharply flavorful dishes. Nice bar, friendly and efficient waitstaff. Owner Paul Kavouksorian helms a fine ship. +$30

Suppenküche 601 Hayes St. (Laguna St.) (415) 252-9289 German. Wirtshaus in the heart of Hayes. Heidi and Hans sitting elbow-to-elbow on family-style wooden tables, noshing on Bavarian specialties like spätzle and wiener schnitzel and washing it all down with malty German ale. Fun place, hearty food. Check the diet at the door. $30

Trader Vic's 555 Golden Gate Ave. (Van Ness Ave.) (415) 775-6300 Tiki Polynesian. Jet-set watering hole back in the '50s, but the times have changed. Requisite bamboo and rattan, complete with masks, music, and outrigger canoe. Hula home of the original Mai Tai (order it the "old way" for extra bad-ass layer of booze). Stick with anything from nuclear reactor-esque wood-fired oven. +$48

Zuni Café 1658 Market St. (Franklin St.) (415) 552-2522 Mediterranean. Superstar chef Judy Rodgers' baby is a sparkler, all right. Famous roast chicken in wood-fired brick oven, dozen briny oysters at the zinc-topped bar, bottle of rosé at a sidewalk table. Supreme people watching—anyone who's anyone is here. SF gastronomical institution, with the urban legends to prove it. +$50
BlackBook

NIGHTLIFE Hayes Valley & Civic Center

Hôtel Biron 45 Rose St. (Market & Gough Sts.) (415) 703-0403. Euro alert! Not quite Barcelona or Paris, but close enough. Tiny cave-like boîte, leather and wrought-iron flourishes, romantic (read: horny and groping) clientele. Good selection of wines and beer, plus cheeses, smoked meats, and caviar for grazing.
BlackBook

Jade Bar 650 Gough St. (McAllister St.) (415) 869-1900 What better place to knock back a few liver-pickling Betty Fords or signature Jade cocktails than in a former AA meetinghouse? Salut! Three narrow floors encompass fish tanks, koi pond, wall-sized waterfall (but is that chlorine we smell?), and shag-carpeted loft full of kitten heels and tube tops. Two-way mirror in the men's room allows for sneak peeks at the action by the bar.

Marlena's 488 Hayes St. (Octavia St.) (415) 864-6672 With the Empress Marlena lording (ladying?) it over the bar, Euro-disco bumping from the speakers, and weekend drag shows and revues (Fauxgirls! cohosted by Victoria Secret) taking over, it's hard for a boy, girl, or anyone to go wrong here. Drinks are cheap, wigs are cheaper.

Place Pigalle 520 Hayes St. (Octavia St.) (415) 552-2671 Gentrification? What gentrification? Artsy types, pool sharks, and neighborhood locals keep it real with beer, wine, or sake cocktails. Subversive art sets the scene around the billiards table. Beware when it's Wild Joe or Bossman behind the eight-ball. **BlackBook**

Rickshaw Stop 155 Fell St. (Van Ness Ave. & Franklin St.) (415) 861-2011 Baby-toting parents (there's a happy hour just for them), unpublished writers, skinny mop-top boys in bands. They all call this cavernous rec room home, at least for a cocktail or three. Fall into one of the plush couches with a Big Olé (Rockstar and vodka) and chow down on the corn-dog special. Foosball table and, yes, rickshaws.

Soluna 272 McAllister St. (Larkin St.) (415) 621-2200 Numb those civic blues with a Pain Killer (Bacardi Coconut, OJ, pineapple juice, coconut). After happy hour and dinner crowds clear, tables are shoved aside for the toned and tanned (relatively speaking, at least) to grind to Euro-house, salsa, and funk.

_____

_____

_____

_____

_____

_____

_____

_____

_____

_____

_____

"Chicago is the great American city, New York is one of the capitals of the world, and Los Angeles

is a constellation of plastic; San Francisco is a lady..." —Norman Mailer

MISSION & BERNAL HEIGHTS (map p. 129-130)

Say you're a nouveau poet, struggling artist, postmodern folk singer, or Burning Man party promoter. We're willing to bet you live in the **Mission**. Slacker irony and self-conscious cool rule the scene in a neighborhood so pulsing with color it spills out into the street, literally—in the form of impromptu poetry slams and power-to-the-people murals and coffeehouses packed with creative angst. As for wardrobe? We're talking vintage, with bedhead to match. You got your New Wave boots and oversized shades? Shrunken T-shirt with self-deprecating slogan? Hit Community Thrift and make sure you're covered. True to the area's Latino roots, taco shops and pupuserias blare screeching mariachi tunes next to newer arrivals like slicker design stores, singles-heavy watering holes, and those neverending small-plate restaurants. Then there's Dave Eggers' 826 Valencia, lording it over the 'hood like a full-sail pirate ship staffed by bushy-tailed volunteers. Eggers is the Mission District's local boy made good, a prince among paupers, an elusive legend of his own making. Watch and learn, son—it could happen to you. Sunny **Bernal** is quite a bit more mellow, home to stoop sales and bookstores and gentle cat-loving souls. Women in overalls hold hands and push Bugaboos up the hill as yapping Jack Russells run amok off leash and the calories keep comin' at **Blue Plate** and **Emmy's**. Check us canoodling under the overpass in the heat of the oven at **Woodward's Garden**, taking on the carne asada challenge at **El Farolito**, getting all loopy with the famous Frank Chu at **12 Galaxies**, and tearing it up, Tito Puente–style, on the dance floor at **El Rio**.

RESTAURANTS Mission & Bernal Heights

Andalu 3198 16th St. (Guerrero St.) (415) 621-2211 Tapas. Small plates! You don't say. Menu starts off in Spain and wanders the globe in search of new concept. Donut holes dipped into Castilian hot chocolate go off. Simple interior can't quite live up to innovative tapas or risqué conversations. Divine sangria. $33

Bissap Baobab 2323 Mission St. (19th & 20th Sts.) (415) 826-9287 Senegalese. West African designer showcase for white folks in that multiculti frame of mind. Thatched mat ceiling and baobab tree sculpture made for Carnival. We're talking world issues to world music over fried plantains and marinated shrimp. Exotic cocktails with fresh tamarind or guava get you liquored up quick! Great for groups, but keep an eye on your date. $18

Blue Plate 3218 Mission St. (29th St.) (415) 282-6777 New American. Like your dream of a perfect restaurant. Counter seating, open kitchen, tattooed chefs improvising on the spot, 'cuz they're badasses like that. New Wave hotties batting their eyelashes. Twinkly garden, too. Get the Blue Plate meatloaf, pork chop, or goat-cheese mac and cheese. And don't skimp on the sides. $32

Boogaloos 3296 22nd St. (Valencia Sts.) (415) 824-4088 Breakfast. Bring us your tired, your weak, your partied-out, and Boogaloos fixes it all with one mean break-fast. Last night's rumpled Mission crawl in trademark thrifts rallying amid colorful mosaic walls and kiddie artwork. Quick—when's the last time you craved a biscuit with vegetarian gravy? Just go with it. $10

Chez Spencer 82 14th St. (Folsom St.) (415) 864-2191 Californian-French. Expense-account dining on sketchy don't-take-the-Jag street. Oddly romantic, soaring industrial space with coveted outdoor garden under heat lamps and sur-real white picket fence. White tablecloths, white asparagus, mostly white people. Heavenly antelope, delectable frog's legs, and spritelike French chef slaving over wood-burning oven. Foie gras on toast with jam—yeah, baby. +$60

Delfina 3621 18th St. (Guererro & Dolores Sts.) (415) 552-4055 Italian. Overly moussed males, technophiles, and high-class hipsters collide in fine dining establish-ment. Art-house backdrop, seasonal menu based on fresh market ingredients. Get any of the homemade pastas and grilled calamari with white bean salad. Multi-pierced yet professional staff unusually spunky and energetic. Must be something in the food. $40

Emmy's Spaghetti Shack 18 Virginia Ave. (Mission St.) (415) 206-2086 Italian. It's Mamma Mia!, Trenchtown Rock, and Petticoat Junction all in one! Tin roof ceiling, vintage aprons on a clothesline, reggae and dancehall on the decks. Rasta lovers and dot-com bombers bouncing back for malt liquor and spaghetti with giant meatballs. Lick-the-bowl-clean good. -$20

Esperpento 3295 22nd St. (Valencia & Mission Sts.) (415) 282-8867 Tapas. Afraid of vampires? Tapas restaurant with full menu of meats, fish, and vegeta-bles, although garlic is the main ingredient. Loud, saucy groups putting down sangria in festive atmosphere. Spicy chicken, grilled mussels, and calamari, if you can handle the garlic extravaganza. Roving mariachi band, of course. $20

Foreign Cinema 2534 Mission St. (21st & 22nd Sts.) (415) 648-7600 Californian. For those nights when the multiplex won't do. New twist on dinner and a movie mobbed by Independent Film Channel addicts and film-noir romantics. Foreign classics and cult favorites projected onto concrete wall, though films are backdrop, not main event. Menu a tad too cute—apps are "premieres" and mains are "features"—but sophisticated and distinctive. Impressive oyster bar. $43

Goood Frickin' Chicken 10 29th St. (Mission St.) (415) 970-2428 Chicken. A bold statement. With a name like that, the bird should do your housework, pay your bills, maybe give you a massage. It's good, just not frickin' goood. Whole chicken, half chicken, or chicken shwarma hovering between moist and dry. Should be called Fairly Decent Chicken. Barren, nondescript interior and blaring Middle Eastern music steer patrons to takeout. $9

Herbivore 983 Valencia St. (20th & 21st Sts.) (415) 826-5657 Vegetarian. Only thing equal to rainbow of vegetables is hair color of patrons. Herbal punks, bike messengers, hippie chicks feasting on inventive vegetarian cuisine. Grilled veggies done just right with dipping sauces. Big, beautiful salads, but do yourself a favor and sidestep the hemp dressing. What is this, the '60s? $15

La Rondalla 901 Valencia St. (Market St.) (415) 647-7474 Mexican. Prom night for Chicano version of Footloose. Twinkle lights, translucent cellophane, tinsel, metallic streamers hanging from ceiling. Lethal margaritas are catalysts for loud and crazy nights. Big groups come for drinks and dinner, stay for drinks and atmosphere. Simple Mexican fare, always served with rice and beans. Mariachi band gets it started, and off it goes till 2 a.m.

La Taqueria 2889 Mission St. (25th St.) (415) 285-7117 Mexican. Part of the great Mission taco debate. Hot griddled beauties oozing with melted cheese and carnitas, chorizo or carne asada hit all the sweet spots. No rice, but we likes 'em better that way anyway. Just beware of the other toppings—one taco with all the fixings will set you back nearly $10. Stucco walls and Mexican murals so you know you're in the barrio. Creamy, cinnamon-y horchata goodness. $12

Levende Lounge 1710 Mission St. (Duboce Ave.) (415) 864-5585. New American. Build your own Bloody Mary bar, for those not too spun out to tell a celery stalk from a green bean. Earnest, endearing mélange of nightclub-cum-restaurant on edges of Mission, next to the overpass. Om Records DJs keep the fluffy house beats going. -$30

Liberty Café & Bakery 410 Cortland Ave. (Bennington & Wool Sts.) (415) 695-8777 American. Little House on Bernal Heights. New moms swapping secrets, moony-eyed couples in love. Comfort food in country-kitchen setting. Fennel and garlic puree soup a must, but potpies have got themselves a rep. Travel down short passage to back garden and little bakery selling savory muffins and insane brioche. By night, bakery becomes a wine bar. $25

Limón 524 Valencia St. (16th & 17th Sts.) (415) 252-0918 Peruvian. A family affair. Brothers Castillo opened this pretty boutique gem, then shipped mama in to do the cooking. Ceviches, parihuela (Peruvian bouillabaisse), Niman Ranch pork chop on bed of cabbage and potato hash. Long waits, lots of noise, lovely nonetheless. Feel-good kinda place. $28

Little Nepal 925 Cortland Ave. (Folsom & Gates Sts.) (415) 643-3881 Nepalese. Little restaurant. Little waiting area. Big flavors. Big following. Menu mixing up Chinese and north Indian food, so anything goes from chow mein to samosas. Abrupt service constantly trying to turn tables. Minimalist interior rings few bells of Nepal (other than map of Everest and snap of Edmund Hillary on the wall), but food and music take you there. $20

Luna Park 694 Valencia St. (18th St.) (415) 553-8584 American. Restaurant as playpen for Gerber babies all grown up. Caramel apple on Popsicle stick? Corn on the cob? Make your own s'mores? What's next, double-dutch? Winner of best DIY drink award: original-recipe Dr Pepper in bottle, small beaker of Absolute Vanilla, vanilla syrup, glass of ice, Dr Pepper-flavored Jelly Bellys all served on a silver platter. Alcoholic chemistry set of our dreams. $31

Moki's Sushi and Pacific Grill 830 Cortland Ave. (Gates & Ellsworth Sts.) (415) 970-9336 Japanese. Hawaiian sushi? Hell, why not? We'll even throw in some Polynesian shit and a few dudes in Aloha shirts. Ecstasy—not just something to do in a club. In this case, a deep-fried sushi roll with maguro, bincho, and avocado. Peach walls, red hibiscus flowers are stylish, but chill. Double dates chowing down to Tracy Chapman in laid-back island atmosphere. $25

Moonlight Café and Crepe House 634 Cortland Ave. (Anderson & Moultrie Sts.) (415) 647-6448 American. Moonlight conspicuously absent here, thanks to 5:30 p.m. close. Crepes, however, in abundant supply. By-the-books creperie (omelets, bagels, and falafel, too), right down to colorful chalk blackboard. Lattes and laptops doing the linger-all-day thing over mediocre screenplays and half-assed attempts at novels. $9

Palace Steak House 3047 Mission St. (Cesar Chavez & 26th Sts.) (415) 647-2011 Steak. Not so palace-like from the outside, with bright yellow signage and worn-out specials hanging in dingy windows. Locals know the royal secret: succulent, perfectly cooked-to-order steaks fit for bluebloods. Steak dinner ringing in at $9.69, with salad, potato, and garlic bread. Veggie burgers and fish too, although why you'd get that here is a mystery. $13

Pakwan 3180 16th St. (Valencia & Guerrero Sts.) (415) 255-2440 Indian. Forget the funeral pyre—when we die, just bathe us in a vat of tikka. Creamy, spicy, smoky chicken tikka masala, to be exact. Order at the counter and wait as they bring it to your bare-bones table. Benghan bhartha, channa masala, sag daal, all dirt-cheap. BYO Kingfisher and get plenty of naan to soak up excess spicy goodness. $12

Taqueria Can-Cun 2288 Mission St. (18th & 19th Sts.) (415) 252-9560; 3211 Mission St. (Fair Ave. & 29th St.) (415) 550-1414 Mexican. Spring break in Tijuana! Ranchero soundtrack included. Hot little Mexican mamacitas and streetwise, gold chain–wearing male counterparts ready for a beat-down if you look at their woman the wrong way. Huge burritos, overflowing cheesy quesadillas with juicy roasted meats, fresh veggies, killer guacamole. Hard-pressed to find a better taco in town. $7

Tokyo Go Go 3174 16th St. (Guererro & Valencia Sts.) (415) 864-2288 Japanese. Visions of Bubblicious dancing through your head. Sprocket-like sushi lovers beneath bubble-shaped lamps in spacey setting of Pop Art pastels. Tuna and salmon tartare with spicy guacamole and shrimp chips, fresher-than-fresh nigiri, East-meets-West rolls like the Azteca (avocado, spicy crab, jalapeños). One, two, three cold sakes to start the night off right. $39

Sunflower Authentic Vietnamese 506 Valencia St. (16th & 17th Sts.) (415) 626-5022 Vietnamese. Simple little Mission gem with well-priced menu. Family-style dining on BBQ pork, salt-and-pepper shrimp, sautéed beef, five-spice chicken, all washed down with cold Vietnamese beer. Fresh veggie and tofu options, too. Little Vietnamese hostess telling girls they look "so skinny!"—clearly knowing how to woo them back. $15

The Last Supper Club 1199 Valencia Street (23rd St.) (415) 695-1199 Italian. Like a greatest-hits collection of Italian-American clichés. You want pennies in the fountain? You want a dark staircase leading down to a library-paneled banquet room? Fuggeddaboudit. Don Corleone meets Paulie Walnuts meets Sharon Stone in Casino. Five-layer lasagna and pork saltimbocca, even spaghetti carbonara for brunch! Washing it all down, we've got a Roman Fling with Aranciata and Prosecco poured over marinated slices of fruit. $28

Walzwerk 381 S. Van Ness Ave. (15th St.) (415) 551-7181 German. Ya wohl meets rock 'n' roll. Authentic and eclectic, thanks to two groovy Berliner lasses cranking out schnitzel, brats, and potato pancakes for artsy Mission pals. Low prices keep the bohos coming, or maybe it's the three East German beers on tap. Sprockets-worthy. $25

We Be Sushi 538 Valencia St. (16th & 17th Sts.) (415) 565-0749; 1071 Valencia St. (21st & 22nd Sts.) (415) 826-0607 Japanese. "Just like mom used to make." Reminiscent of a bank lobby—marble floors, dark wood, Western landscapes, buttoned-down folks discussing sensible issues. Reliably delicious sushi/sashimi. Young crowd, chill music. $16

Woodward's Garden 1700 Mission St. (Duboce St.) (415) 621-7122 Cal-Med. Feel like you're at the speedway, watching cars rush to the freeway? Outside is permanent construction site, and front room can get kind of hot. But consider calm and cozy back room, kind server, affable quasi-intellectual clientele, and hearty-seasonal-heirloom-organic fare winning everlasting raves. Romance under the overpass. $35 **BlackBook**

NIGHTLIFE Mission & Bernal Heights

Amnesia 853 Valencia St. (19th & 20th Sts.) (415) 970-0012 Asymmetrical '80s chicks, worker bees, adorable tattooed gay boys chilling in red, brothel-like surroundings. Fine selection of local beers and saucy sangria. DJs and bands (remember when they broke Deerhoof?), plus Tuesday-night karaoke that can't get any better. Guys in seersucker and camo you'd swear were channeling Journey accompanied by karaoke dude wailing on bitchin' cardboard guitar.

Beauty Bar 2299 Mission St. (19th St.) (415) 285-0323 Not so bad, as theme bars go. Babes in stylish toques trying hard to look nonchalant. Spinoff of NYC bar in real beauty salon, only this one just fronts it. Gold salon chairs with dryers, sparkly red walls lined with Toni home perms and tonics, lethal-looking Prell-colored cocktails. Manicure and martini for $10 during happy hour gets you drunk and pretty at the same time.

Bruno's 2389 Mission St. (20th St.) (415) 648-7701 Jazz hot, daddy-o. Wear that zoot suit and saunter on in. Recently renovated '50s supper-club aura via deep red leather booths and 500-gallon fish tank, Mingus Amungus and the dazzling Marcus Shelby Jazz Orchestra swinging with the best of them. Late-night, semi-illicit bad behavior in the Green Room upstairs. **BlackBook**

Cama 3192 16th St. (Guerrero St.) (415) 864-5255 Dated Euro concept (beds in a bar!) lives on. Cave-like lounge where design matches crowd: electro-alterna-queer-skater-funky, all going to hell on the weekend. Bed chambers apparently designed with Catherine the Great and Satan himself in mind. Superior cocktails, preciously named and steeply priced. Will sell liquor to go—the better to seal the deal with trashy hookup on the smoking patio. ✴

Casanova 527 Valencia St. (16th & 17th Sts.) (415) 863-9328 Mission lounge swathed in red, or weird store hawking light fixtures? You tell us. Eclectic estate-sale lamps, mostly of the bunched-grape variety. Gotta love the black-velvet paintings around bar. Decent jukebox, fairly strong drinks. Not many Latin lovers to go around, but plenty of penniless freelance writers to spare.

Chaise Lounge 309 Cortland Ave. (Bocana St.) (415) 401-0952 Finally—a lesbian bar that's neither Western nor dive. Open to everyone, even the dogs. Intimate vintage-decked boite with "kissing room" in back for Craigslist blind dates ready to take it to next level. Friday Quench party equals sex toy contests, dancing bar girls, drag king singalongs, ladies'-night vibe. Yowza. ☆

Dalva 3121 16th St. (Albion St.) (415) 252-7740 Bar by candlelight. You're here on Wednesdays for the excellent Red Wine Sessions, starring XLR8R columnist and DJ Toph One, with special guest appearances by the likes of Tommy Guerrero. Straight-up party music, no foolin' around. No dance floor, but when did that ever stop you? Off the hook and hella tight.

Delirium Cocktails 3139 16th St. (Valencia & Guerrero Sts.) (415) 552-5525 Remember in Pretty in Pink when Blaine went into the courtyard to ask Andie for a date? Pretty much that same crowd. Here we are in the new millennium, but it seems no one told Delirium. Like a Virgins, Flocks of Seagulls, Pet Shop Boys putting mod outfits on parade. Couples slow-dancing to the Cure. Rad.

Doc's Clock 2575 Mission St. (21st & 22nd Sts.) (415) 824-3627 Shuffleboard kinda like Nana and Poppa on their senior cruise, but played by girls with retro bangs and boys with retro kicks instead. We'll clock your doc, alright! Only margarita outside of a Mexican joint guaranteed to knock you on your ass. Man behind the decks plays the room just right—easy to chat, easy to groove.

El Rio 3158 Mission St. (Valencia St.) (415) 282-3325 Here is where we all get down. This is how we do it. Don't care who you are, gay or straight, rich or poor, from 3 to 8 p.m. on Salsa Sundays, you are a dancing fool. Fabulous cross-section of SF society getting hot and bothered to the sounds of local salsa outfits on the patio. Other nights, you've got world beat (Fridays) and punk rock (Wednesdays). Truly, something for all.

Elbo Room 647 Valencia St. (17th & 18th Sts.) (415) 552-7788 Double your pleasure. Mixed bag of disheveled thirtysomethings rocking their Goodwill and harkening back to fierce arcade days with Ms. Pacman and Donkey Kong Jr. But kicked up a notch, 'cuz boy can they booze. Two pool tables round out game-room Olympics. Music junkies head upstairs for entirely different scene of Afrobeat, samba, funk bands and DJs. Don't be afraid to get crazy, now.

Latin American Club 3286 22nd St. (Valencia & Mission Sts.) (415) 647-2732 Not terribly Latin American, but faded piñatas hanging from ceiling are a gesture, at least. Entire wall papered with screaming political statements in red and black. Early evening brings vinyl geeks from Aquarius Records around the corner drooling on latest Japanese imports. By late evening, blurry-eyed singles in the midst of desperate and unusual courting measures.

Lexington Club 3464 19th St. (Valencia & Mission Sts.) (415) 863-2052 Hot young lesbian scene is smokin'! Tongue-pierced baby dykes making eyes at each other to sexy jukebox soundtrack of De La Soul. Guys, forget about getting in unless you're bringing some womyn with ya. Now behave.

Lone Palm 3394 22nd St. (Guerrero & Valencia Sts.) (415) 648-0109 Classiest dive in town. Channeling Nick and Nora, not to mention Bogie and Bacall, as you sip your martini and light up (bartender turns a blind eye). Dim atmosphere, white table linens provide the class. Johnny Cash, White Stripes, denim-clad patrons come through for the dive. Art-house dreamers debating civic crisis with fierce integrity and drinking to get drunk, dammit.

Phone Booth 1398 S. Van Ness Ave. (25th St.) (415) 648-4683 Free popcorn, bullfighting tapestries, pitchers of Pabst, Barbie chandelier. All this, in a no-man's-land far from civilization, with assorted collection of weirdos, barflies, rockers, and gays. Random SF nightlife at its finest.

Pink 2925 16th St. (S. Van Ness Ave.) (415) 431-8889 Pretty Pac Heights junior socialites and aging club kids getting down to business in posh little cotton-candy nook owned by SF house fixture Frankie Boissy. Remember his birthday party when he appeared all in white dressed like Jesus? Formerly known as Liquid, with coterie of naysayers who liked it better that way.

Roccapulco Supper Club 3140 Mission St. (Cesar Chavez St. & Coso Ave.) (415) 648-6611 Gloria Estefan was right: The rhythm is going to get you. Salsa enthusiasts and dirty-dancing hopefuls spicing up Bernal Heights nightlife at neon palm tree–lined fiesta. Friday and Saturday nights bring fiery Latino instructors conducting salsa classes. Live music every weekend. Strictly enforced dress code, so break out the cummerbund, pomade, and pencil-thin mustache.

SOUTH

MISSION & BERNAL HEIGHTS

Skip's Tavern 453 Cortland Ave. (Andover & Wool Sts.) (415) 282-3456 Epitome of neighborhood dive, complete with long-haired Clerks types trying in vain to woo passing women inside. Originally a pool hall, still a shrine to the game, with prominently displayed trophies and tournament signup sheets. Marilyn Monroe and 49ers given prime real estate with posters and knickknacks squeezed onto every inch of wall space. Live jazz and blues nightly, weekly R&B jam sessions.

Skylark 3089 16th St. (Valencia & Mission Sts.) (415) 621-9294 They say Skylark is wanker slang for going out with your mates and getting pished. Indeed. Strong drinks, sexy ambiance, good music make for a rather excellent place to get hammered with loved ones. House, soul, funk, jazz nightly, often spun by fit DJ birds.

12 Galaxies 2565 Mission St. (21st & 22nd Sts.) (415) 970-9777 Small enough to feel intimate, big enough to kick ass. Groovy live-music venue, i.e. Sleepytime Gorilla Museum and True Skool Presents. Name comes from Frank Chu, a bizarre character spotted around town with political/extraterrestrial-conspiracy message boards. Chu sometimes turns up, message board in hand.

26 Mix 3024 Mission St. (26th & Cesar Chavez Sts.) (415) 826-7378 Large bar for heavy drinking, small club for getting down, video-game haven for high scorers. Trucker hat, dreadlocks, or fauxhawk required. Hip-hop, funk, house, what have you, and regulars shaking whatever God gave them. Nuzzle in a velvet booth to the romantic stylings of experimental '70s porn.

Wild Side West 424 Cortland Ave. (Andover & Wool Sts.) (415) 647-3099 Old Western movie with lesbian twist. Kitschy/charming Bernal Heights destination for local ladies. Plethora of softball and pool trophies shows they take extracurricular activities seriously. Eclectic décor includes: cigar store Indian, funky shrine to women's shoes, wooden parrot holding a Corona. Balcony like your friend's house. Resident musician plays Blackbird on acoustic guitar as women smoke and snuggle.

Zeitgeist 199 Valencia St. (Duboce Ave.) (415) 255-7505 Leather-clad bikers, Critical Massers, Mission slacks, Marina yuppies, and the tamale lady making the rounds—a literal smorgasbord. Testosterone runs high as dudes challenge each other to a drinkoff. Huge patio garden in back with picnic benches and BBQ to punk, rawk, and country tunes. And a guesthaus, too!? When all's said and done, a fine place to fritter away the day.

"You are fortunate to live here. If I were your President,

I would levy a tax on you for living in San Francisco!" —Mikhail Gorbachev

CASTRO & NOE VALLEY (map p. 131)

All aboard the gay amusement park ride! D&G tank tops and tight Versus jeans required. **Pretty boys and their fan clubs rule the roost in the Castro**, with the requisite bistros and bars and muscle shops to supply their every whim. Rippling male torsos proliferate here, along with husky-voiced Jodie Foster look-alikes on the dance floor at **The Cafe** and silver-haired leather daddies congregating at, well, **Daddy's**. The high-maintenance brigade get their Queer Eye–approved shave cream at Nancy Boy, their Rogan at Rolo, their spray tans at Tan Bella, and their erotic greeting cards at Does Your Father Know? (Nope, chances are he doesn't.) The giant Wurlitzer rises and falls with panache at the Castro Theatre before the 8 p.m. showing of Valley of the Dolls (audience participation to be expected), while Abercrombie understudies pass the picket lines at Badlands for pop and PNP hookups. **Just remember: Fierce is a state of mind.** One hill over, **Noe Valley is full of starter homes for breeders**, with 24th Street as its shopping mecca with quaint New Age slant. **Brunch is an art form, whether you're getting your eggs at Miss Millie's or Savor.** There's a subtle femme-on-femme pickup scene afoot, but it's more on the Basic Instinct side of things. We're digging the terrarium vibe at Cafe Flore, the stone crabs and supper-club scene at **Mecca**, and the show tunes at **Martuni's** in preparation for our alcohol-soaked, adrenaline-fueled, Scissor Sisters–inspired debut at **The Mint**. Clearly, it's that kind of neighborhood.

RESTAURANTS Castro & Noa Valley

Anchor Oyster Bar 579 Castro St. (19th St.) (415) 431-3990 Seafood. Hello, big sailor! Packing in Castro crowd and Japanese tourists at marble counter since 1977 for swimmingly fresh bowls of Boston clam chowder. Faint smell of sea not coming from stuffed sea bass on wall. Tablemates seduce with oysters on the half shell. $22

Blue 2337 Market St. (Noe St.) (415) 863-2583 American. Buff boys in muscle shirts gobbling mac and cheese to the musical stylings of Jewel. We're not making this stuff up. Like being in a submarine eating tuna casserole with Ritz-cracker crumbles. If we'd known, we would have joined the Navy years ago. $20

Chloe's 1399 Church St. (26th St.) (415) 648-4116 American. Burberry beach hats and L.L. Bean Boat and Totes lunching on dill egg salad on rosemary toast. Sometimes brunching on smoked-salmon scrambled eggs and pecan pancakes. Sign up on yellow sheet and peruse the blackboard specials, 'cuz it's gonna be a while. $15

Chow 215 Church St. (Market St.) (415) 552-2469 American. Behind velvet curtain awaits vamped-up culinary version of Mayberry. No Ron Howard, but Sunday meat-ball sandwich draws loyal crowd, as does iceberg wedge with buttermilk blue-cheese dressing. Muffled chatter and clanking plates keep regulars alert. Cap off with warm chocolate cake à la mode to add a little pot to your belly. $20

Côté Sud 4238 18th St. (Collingwood & Diamond Sts.) (415) 255-6565 French. Let's play a game. We hold hands across the table, act all snuggly over the $25 prix-fixe special, and pretend we're Vanessa and Billy from Pac Heights. Haven't you always wanted to get cozy over duck confit and crème brulée? Chef Eric Lanvert supplies quack and crème. All that's left to do is cop a little feel. +$35

Eric's Restaurant 1500 Church St. (27th St.) (415) 282-0919 Hunan/Mandarin. Much better-than-average Chinese with fresh Cali flavors. Mango prawns, Hunan lamb, hot-and-sour soup ladled tableside. Airy Victorian with big bay windows on street corner next to flower stand. So charming we hard-ly need to eat. -$16

Fattoush 1361 Church St. (Clipper & 26th Sts.) (415) 641-0678 Middle Eastern. Shorts and T-shirt crowd of UC Berkeley grad dropouts. Minced lamb and skew-ered chicken never tasted so good. Backyard patio, even. Mediterranean brunch scramble of spinach, feta, olives, and almonds cancels out bad easy listening inflicted upon walk though main dining room. -$25

Firefly 4288 24th St. (Douglass St.) (415) 821-7652 Fusion. Thank goodness the babysitter showed, otherwise we'd be spoon-feeding Cheerios to little Tyler instead of filling up on this hearty osso buco. I told her we wouldn't be home till 10, so let's go wild with the cream pie. Sugar and carbs! Oh, I feel so naughty in my sweater set and pearls. +$34

Hahn's Hibachi 1305 Castro St. (Jersey & 24th Sts.) (415) 642-8151 Korean. That's not your mom wearing Old Navy polar fleece, it just looks a hell of a lot like her. Family-owned biz next door to nail salon. This place smells cooked. It's all about the BBQ, from short ribs to eel. $18

Hamano Sushi 1332 Castro St. (Jersey & 24th Sts.) (415) 826-0825 Japanese. Yuppies complain about lack of bar space. Big deal. They don't look too unhappy checking themselves out in the mirror while chowing down on $7 lunch combos. Huge selection of nigiri and maki rolls, sharp smell of fish keeping it fresh all around. -$20

Herb's Fine Foods 3991 24th St. (Noe & Sanchez Sts.) (415) 826-8937 American. Mom-and-pop diner, little red and white gingham curtains, old-timey feel. Will it be the pancake sandwich (one egg, two strips bacon, two hotcakes) or the 2x4 (two eggs, four hotcakes)? How about coffee and a daily special? Locals hit it as early as 6:30 a.m. $15

Home 2100 Market St. (Church St.) (415) 503-0333 American. White wainscoting and kitschy early-bird specials draw Martha's Vineyard groupies, even on site of old Boston Market. Fancied-up country-fried chicken and sides of mac and cheese go down way too easy with a French martini. Smell of meat and background yammering keep things lively as clustered crowd waiting for tables scans for ex-lovers in disguise. -$25

La Mediterranée 288 Noe St. (Market St.) (415) 431-7210 Mediterranean. Chicken pomegranate, rolled levant sandwiches, honey-drizzled baklava help ease all pain. Sidewalk seating and Django Reinhardt—now that feels good. And that stained-glass mermaid is wagging her tail your way. Quit whining and eat your dolmas. $20

Le Zinc 4063 24th St. (Castro & Noe Sts.) (415) 647-9400 French. Petite piece of Paris on left coast. Freelancers bordering on unemployed kill prime working hours over nicoise salad and croque monsieur while Norah Jones works it out. Owners know their vin (they did own a wine bar in Paris, duh), concentrating on French with some California thrown in for good measure. Cassoulet, catfish, couscous. Ooh la la! +$38

Luna 558 Castro St. (18th & 19th Sts.) (415) 621-2566 American. Diehard Cirque du Soleil fans find peace with good mimosas. Heated patio dining with paisley vinyl coverlets on round tables keep the boys happy, as do the eggs florentine and chorizo scramble. We're talking about brunch here, hello! You listening to me or checking out that houseboy? $20

Mecca 2029 Market St. (Church & Dolores Sts.) (415) 621-7000 New American. Look, there goes Trevor Traina. And isn't that Rosario Dawson and the cast of Rent? Supper club goes industrial, with trim Versace-clad boys and slim air-kissing girls. Round bar with Mylar screens that let you see out, not in. Love that. Day boat scallops with fava bean purée, seared Hudson Valley foie gras. Another fresh cherry caipirosca, please! +$50 **BlackBook**

Miss Millie's 4123 24th St. (Castro & Diamond Sts.) (415) 285-5598 American. Why anyone would want to get on the giant scale is beyond us.

Especially after buttermilk biscuits with sausage gravy or lemon ricotta pancakes with blueberry syrup. Overly crowded brunch spot, but don't let slight grandma feel and windowboxes scare you off. Good place to eat away Saturday-morning hangover. $19

Orphan Andy's 3991 17th St. (Market & Castro Sts.) (415) 864-9795 American. What a difference 18 hours can make. By day, nice folks eating tuna melts with fries. By night, well, take a chance and find out for yourself. And then let us know why a 7-oz. steak is on the diet plate. Open 24 hours, free refills on 20-oz. sodas, giant monarch overhead, tweaky club kids. And they said there was no nightlife in SF. $12

Savor 3913 24th St. (415) 282-0344 (Sanchez & Noe Sts.) Fusion. Michael Jackson on the radio, pah-leeze! Patio area sorta resembles suburban mall, but most diners probably heading to Target in Daly City anyway. Crepes are the way to go—the Kyoto, with grilled tofu and shiitake mushrooms, or the Santa Fe, chicken apple sausage and scrambled eggs. Yum. -$17

Tallula 4230 18th St. (Collingwood St.), (415) 437-6722 Indian-French fusion. More Bankhead than Bollywood. Quirky and hip romance in old Victorian, with bohème waiters getting a workout on spiral staircases. Cozy downstairs lounge serves challengingly flavored cocktails (licorice and lemon?), plus small plates of borderline chi-chi cuisine. Saffron walls and mother-of-pearl mobiles make for evocative mood, despite pokey service and uneven food. $36

2223 2223 Market St. (Sanchez St.) (415) 431-0692 American. Personal trainers getting off shifts at Gold's add some muscle to the mix. Southern-fried chicken salad and smoked salmon benedict for legendary brunch in contemporary space that feels very West Coast. Sublime onion rings. Even rich queens love the weeknight $29.95 tasting menu—three courses and that grilled flatbread you've heard so much about. +$35 **BlackBook**

NIGHTLIFE Castro & Noa Valley

Amber 718 14th St. (Church St.) (415) 626-7827 Relax, you're not breaking the law. Cool and moody lounge where smoking is OK. So you don't have to huddle in the doorway to light up, and if you're looking to buy a $5 "nudie" glass, you're in the right place. Chill amber lighting, Wednesday '80s nights, specialty cocktail with peach schnapps and 7Up.

SOUTH

CASTRO & NOE VALLEY

The Bar 456 Castro St. (18th & Market Sts.) (415) 626-7220 After catching oldie but goodie at The Castro Theatre, step across the street where a youngish gay crowd shouts over blaring disco. Tables suspended like IKEA-cum-Star Trek Enterprise gone wrong, with everything cast in red. Just sci-fi enough for our liking. Two-for-one well drinks during happy hour make us happy cruisin' Castro campers.

Bliss Bar 4026 24th St. (Noe & Castro Sts.) (415) 826-6200 Oasis of cool in stroller-centric neighborhood. Just overlook the rude bartender because they're playing good down tempo. Cage room in back with faux Jackson Pollock is where it's at. Order 24th Street cosmo with Smirnoff triple sec and cranberry, but move on to martinis before handing out digits.

The Café 2367 Market St. (Castro St.) (415) 861-3846 Six-hour happy hour is what they have in mind. Covered terrace turns beyond packed Friday and Saturday nights with Castro girls and boys looking for love in all the wrong places. More happening from the outside, but pool table, DJ, and fun 'n' horny crowd justify hanging for a while. No shirtless dancing, please. Best place to watch SF Pride parade.

Café Du Nord 2170 Market St. (Church & Sanchez Sts.) (415)-861-5016 All dark wood and good ghost energy floating around. 1907 speakeasy even has secret door used by gangsters to escape cops. They say copper strips on the bar deflected bullets. Eclectic, to say the least—Liz Phair one night and casino games the next. Maine crab cakes soak up all the liquor.

Café Flore 2298 Market St. (16th & Noe Sts.) (415) 621-8579. So they play the same spiritual music as your acupuncturist. We don't care, we like it. Neighborhood institution kinda like being in a greenhouse, except with espresso machine and decent beer selection. Bathroom is so Amtrak. Colorful cross-section of Castro young and groovy giving you the eye. **BlackBook**

Daddy's 440 Castro St. (18th St.) (415) 621-8732 Not to be confused with Who's Your Daddy, near the Tenderloin. This one's for the leather-loving set, not exactly a casual drink spot. Dark little hole brings the men in chaps out for action, though hardly of the father-son variety. Beefcake.

The Dubliner 3838 24th St. (Vicksburg & Church Sts.) (415) 826-2279 More sports bar than Irish pub, despite the name. Thirteen TVs with drag racing, poker, and baseball leave Noe residents little to complain about. Kools for sale, along with little packs of crispy bar snacks. Everything A-OK.

Lucky 13 2140 Market St. (Church & Sanchez Sts.) (415) 487-1313 Saturday barbecue on back patio is just what we had in mind. We like having our smoke and drinking our $2 PBR. Dig the tattoos and punk jukebox, not so much the weekend B&Ts and SF State coeds getting blotto on lemon drops.

Martuni's 4 Valencia St. (Market St.) (415) 241-0205 Chocolate and watermelon martinis, yum. Like Jolly Rancher in a glass. Owner Skip Ziobron still cocktailing it up eight years later. Piano and open mic bring the kids from Hairspray and The Lion King and that 80-year-old guy named Roberto all the locals know. Transgender, gay, straight—it's one big beautiful mixed Martuni world.

The Mint 1942 Market St. (Laguna & Duboce Sts.) (415) 626-4726 Camera pans in: Potbellied man onstage singing "Summer Lovin'," basset hound licking up spilled drink from overzealous bar hug, 301-page songbook with words to "The Rose." Close up on sign: The Mint. Like we need to tell you. Karaoke lounge keeps Friskies behind the cash register. Why? No idea. Do as the locals do. Drink too much, pick cheeseball tune, belt it out like a brave little boy. **BlackBook**

Pilsner Inn 225 Church St. (15th & Market Sts.) (415) 621-7058 No one seems able to explain the penguins and trophies, but that's OK. We like a little mystery. Local crowd that gets three-deep on the weekends, friendly pickup scene on patio, cool SF Pool league members on Tuesday nights. One of the best gay bars in town.

Samovar Tea Lounge 498 Sanchez St. (18th St.) (415) 626-4700 Even hardcore cocktail sluts need a break. We feel all righteous choosing from white, green, oolong, and herbals instead of vodka, rum, or gin. Not a sex club, but a hot bev that promises to help "penetrate" and "dissolve" your issues. Rattan floor, stone Buddha, and sweet smell of tea leave us more blissed-out than three gin-and-tonics.

Twin Peaks Tavern 401 Castro St. (Market St.) (415) 864-9470 Somewhere over the rainbow, way up high... That's Twin Peaks they're singing about. For more than 30 years, it's been home base on Castro Street, spreading the love to the community and those just visiting. Get cozy on grandma pillows lining window seats for killer views of this glorious neighborhood.

The Valley Tavern 4054 24th St. (Noe & Castro Sts.) (415) 285-0674 Friendly and uncool, just like bad hair day. Countless beers on tap. Microbrews. Smoking room. Futurama on the TV. Kenny Loggins on the sound system. Guys doing dorky dance to B-52's. Pool table. ATM. Carding 32-year-old guidebook writer who orders Coca-Cola. Yeah.

SOUTH

CASTRO & NOE VALLEY

Whiskey Lounge 4063 18th St. (Hartford & Castro Sts.) (415) 255-2733 We feel so "in the know" in this "clubby dark space" that serves up "painted ponies, side-cars and rob roys." "Order up the Fuzzy Dick to get in the Castro spirit." Sorry, thought this was Zagats for a minute.

_____

_____

_____

_____

_____

_____

_____

_____

_____

_____

_____

_____

_____

_____

_____

_____

"Money lives in New York. Power sits in Washington. Freedom sips Cappuccino

in a sidewalk cafe in San Francisco." —Joe Flower

RICHMOND & SUNSET (map p. 132-135)

Here we are out in the avenues, where the fog rolls in something awful. What lies beneath? **A multilingual enclave with sleeper foodie ambitions, a bumper crop of Irish bars, and a beach that kicks ass.** Yeah, parking sucks, nightlife's crap, and it's a hell of a lot sunnier on the other side of town. But look close and stick with it—this area delivers. For starters, there's the stupefying selection of round-the-world eats: piroshki at **Katia's**, chicken bastilla at **Aziza**, sweetbreads at **Chapeau**!, tea leaf salad at **Burma Super Star**. Then there's Golden Gate Park, home to buffalo and pagodas and a sprawling conservatory with Little Shop of Horrors–style plants. That rusty-looking pile of metal with an air-traffic control tower? That's our new **De Young Museum**, courtesy of two crazy Swiss architects and a whole bunch of rich folks with dollars to burn. **Ocean Beach is more about drama, not sand.** Check those demon surfers braving the ball-busting temperatures and blowing out their eardrums in the wind tunnel under the **Golden Gate Bridge**. And way out yonder, 27 miles offshore, are the Farallon Islands, where sea birds screech and sharks frolic in the ocean lopping the heads off seals. Just so you know what you're dealing with, now. We'll be pawing at our po'boy over a cold one at **Cajun Pacific**, giving props to the dumpling at **Ton Kiang**, playing Confucius says at **RoHan Lounge**, and grilling that bulgogi something proper at **Brother's**.

RESTAURANTS Richmond & Sunset

Aziza 5800 Geary Blvd. (22nd Ave.) (415) 752-2222. Moroccan. Gourmet show-stopper, thanks to wunderkind chef/owner Mourad Lahlou. Garish painted arch-ways and belly dancer gyrating to blaring music, but it works. Dried fruits, olives, preserved lemon, and almonds add up to winning flavor combinations. Couscous is steamed for eight hours, chicken bastilla rules. +$40 **BlackBook**

Beach Chalet 1000 Great Highway (415) 386-8439 American. Tourist attraction notable mainly for location at western edge of Golden Gate Park, across from Ocean Beach. Cool 1930s WPA frescoes of working men and women near entrance. Knock-'em-dead views of Pacific, good microbrews, but average, over-priced food. Taco Tuesdays, Friday beer and blues. $35

Brother's Korean Restaurant 4128 Geary Blvd. (5th Ave.) (415) 387-7991 Korean. If you're looking for ambiance, look elsewhere. But if it's spicy-good Korean barbecue you're after, plus all the kimchee trimmings, this place delivers. Interactive fun on cook-it-yourself charcoal grills make it good place for a first date. Open till 2 a.m. $25

Burma Super Star 309 Clement St. (4th Ave.) (415) 387-2147 Burmese. Memorable, exotic flavors bridging Chinese, Indian, and Thai, in slightly faded room dominated by Asian arts and crafts. Great samosas, eggplant curry, tea-leaf salad, homemade noodles with duck. Line forms outside, so bring a warm sweater (especially in August). Everyone from couples out on inexpensive dates to large, raucous groups. $20

Cajun Pacific 4542 Irving St. (46th St.) (415) 504-6652 Cajun. Hole in the wall way out by the beach with great gumbo, jambalaya, and etouffee. Beer is cold, tables and walls are covered with old New Orleans music memorabilia, and zydeco on the stereo ties it together. Like a dream about the French Quarter, but with surfers munching on po' boys at next table. Limited hours and days, so call ahead. -$20 **BlackBook**

Carousel 2750 Sloat Blvd. (46th Ave.) (415) 564-6052 Fast Food. Used to be a Doggie Diner, and still has oversized dog's head outside. Greasy burgers and fries, too-high prices, surly and impersonal service. Only reason to come here is to see the Doggie head, now planted on a median strip down the block, so might as well save your money and drive by on your way to somewhere else. $12

Chapeau! 1408 Clement St. (15th Ave.) (415) 750-9787 French. Nicely executed bistro classics (sweetbreads, duck confit, cassoulet) take backseat to outstanding wine list (almost 300 bottles strong). Chatty couple Philippe and Ellen Gardelle make nice-nice throughout dining room. Check comes in a chapeau (!), what else? +$30

Clementine 126 Clement St. (2nd Ave.) (415) 387-0408 French. Who says the Richmond isn't elegant? High-end, bustling little eatery with none of the pretentiousness. Excellent food and service in warm and mellow room. Menu trots out all the standards: escargots, boeuf bourgignon, tarte tatin... +$45

Cliff House/Sutro's 1090 Point Lobos Ave. (415) 386-3330 American. Newly renovated, so ye olde outdated vibe is gone. What's left: killer ocean view, crowd of bluehairs, and slack-jawed tourists in sandals hoping for seal sightings. Dine at Sutro's if grandma's paying, or burgers and crab cakes at the bistro if you're on your own dime. Stick to lunch or early sunset dinner. $50 ★

Ebisu 1283 9th Ave. (Irving St.) (415) 566-1770 Japanese. Very good sushi, but you're not the only one who knows it. No reservations means you'll wait in line that snakes round the corner for salmon teriyaki, lightly battered tempura, and in-the-know favorite salad of octopus, maguro, and hamachi. Narrow, crowded space with exotic lanterns and pagoda roof. Kampai! $32

Goemon Japanese Restaurant 1524 Irving St. (16th Ave.) (415) 664-2288 Japanese. Chuckle as you pass hungry hordes in front of Ebisu on your way to this sleeper surprise. Tasty sushi, generously sliced, in two dining rooms plus small sushi bar. Back room looks out onto Japanese garden and pond. $30

Hotei 1290 9th Ave. (Irving St.) (415) 753-6045 Japanese. Traditional Inner Sunset noodle house across from sister restaurant Ebisu serving soba, ramen, udon, gyoza, and other Japanese specialties. Calming interior and gentle gurgling fountain would make for meditative dining experience, if it weren't for all the hustle. $20

Katia's: A Russian Tearoom 600 5th Ave. (Balboa St.) (415) 668-9292 Russian. Home cooking just like Svetlana used to make, to tune of gently strumming live guitar. Perfectly flaky piroshki, blini with salmon roe and sour cream, beet borscht with rye bread. Large parties of Russian immigrants waxing nostalgic about the homeland. $30

Khan Toke Thai House 5937 Geary Blvd. (24th Ave.) (415) 668-6654 Thai. Longtime neighborhood fixture, decent fare, ornate temple-like décor and fun, festive atmosphere (goes off for family gatherings and birthdays). Staff in traditional Thai garb usher patrons to sunken carved teak tables. Wear clean socks, because your shoes are coming off. $25

Nan King Road Bistro 1360 9th Ave. (Judah & Irving Sts.) (415) 753-2900 Pan-Asian. Hip, industrial-ish interior seems more at home in SoMa than among generic-looking joints in Inner Sunset. Friendly staff, low prices, better-than-average Asian fare with fresh California ingredients, as in green salad with five-spice tofu topped with peanuts and fried ginger. $25

Park Chalet 1000 Great Highway (415) 386-8439 American. Behind sister restaurant Beach Chalet, little bit slicker, but with similar menu—meaning don't come here for food alone. Glass walls and ceiling equal greenhouse effect. Nice oversized fireplace and view of woods at edge of Golden Gate Park. $28

Park Chow 1240 9th Ave. (Lincoln Way & Irving St.) (415) 665-9912 American. Quirky microbrews on tap, roaring fire, and heat lamps in outdoor seating area come over all warm and easy. Lively, inexpensive place to sate your hunger with roast chicken or juicy burger after a day roaming Golden Gate Park. $18

Pizzetta 211 211 23rd Ave. (California St.) (415) 379-9880 Italian. Tiny, off-the-beaten-path gem specializing in cracker-thin-crust pizzas, artisanal cheese plates, and exotic salads. Fine spot for quiet date, if you can bear the wait. Sit outside on the right night—a warm one, with stars—and you'd swear the place was enchanted. $22 **BlackBook**

PJ's Oyster Bed 737 Irving St. (9th Ave.) (415) 566-7775 Cajun/Creole Seafood. Cast-iron skillet shellfish roasts and two-pound platter of crayfish bring on finger-lickin' fun. Delicious Louisiana fare but somewhat pricey, crowded, and noisy. Corporate types next to UCSF students being treated by visiting parents. Give yourself time to find parking, if you fail, try 9th Avenue between Irving and Lincoln. $35

Q 225 Clement St. (3rd Ave.) (415) 752-2298 American. Young, fun crowd in funky comfort-food haven. Mac-and-cheese topped with tater tots, BBQ ribs with baked beans. Exposed kitchen, quirky art, kiddie games built into tables and walls. Table with tree growing through it adds to playhouse effect. $25

Tommy's Mexican 5929 Geary Blvd. (23rd Ave.) (415) 387-4747 Mexican. Loud, bright, crowded cantina with mediocre food. But hey, it's not the food you're here for, it's the tequila. Bar is as jam-packed as rush hour, but margarita makes it a lot more fun than your morning commute. Possibly largest tequila selection in the country (more than 200) and legendary Blue Agave Club. $25

Ton Kiang 5821 Geary Blvd. (22nd Ave.) (415) 387-8273 Chinese. One of the best dim sum places in town, which is saying something. Big, bright place with nothing-special décor—but you'll be too focused on pork buns and shrimp balls to care. Hakka specialties (salt-baked chicken, sizzling rice soup). Lots of Chinese families, so you know this joint is good. +$25

NIGHTLIFE Richmond & Sunset

The Canvas Gallery, Café & Lounge 1200 9th Ave. (Lincoln Way) (415) 504-0060 Is it a bar? Coffee shop? Sandwich shop? Art gallery? Live performance venue? The answer is yes. Big, architecturally interesting room with soaring ceiling, exposed steel beams, lots of blond wood. Neighborhood students plug in laptops or hit the books during the day, then give way to artsy types after dark. **BlackBook**

Fireside Bar 603 Irving St. (7th Ave.) (415) 731-6433 Deep red walls, glowing gas fireplace, and good local art take this up a couple of notches from your typical neighborhood hang. Everyone from middle-aged locals to youngsters out for cocktails.

540 Club 540 Clement St. (6th Ave.) (415) 752-7576 How to make a 540 Club: Take one local dive, add trippy lighting, Catholic School Karaoke Parties, and DJs spinning old-school punk and dirty breaks. Every neighborhood should have one, but you're probably better off in SoMa for this kind of vibe.

Ireland's 32 3920 Geary Blvd. (3rd Ave.) (415) 386-6173 Irish bar wearing its IRA sympathies proudly, in the form of posters and such relating to the Troubles. Live music of the bar-band variety. Mega-crowded on weekend nights, with plenty of young Irish lads and lasses in the mix.

Last Day Saloon 406 Clement St. (5th Ave.) (415) 387-6343 Downstairs room filled with pool tables, dartboards, heavy frat-party vibe. Upstairs cover charge and schedule full of jam bands—hey, it's a frat party with live music! Keep an eye out for musicians on the rise sneaking through town before making a national splash. Etta James, Michael Franti, Big Head Todd & the Monsters—all have played here.

Mucky Duck 1315 9th Ave. (Irving & Judah Sts.) (415) 661-4340 Lovably plain neighborhood dive with good game face. Regulars know how to while away an afternoon running a healthy tab and watching the Giants or Niners. Or Warriors, or did they move to Vegas or something?

The Plough and Stars 116 Clement St. (2nd Ave.) (415) 751-1122 None of the McPub feel you get at most other Irish bars in the Richmond. Long, shadowy room, warm atmosphere, traditional Irish music—none of those drum-machine-and-U2-cover bands. Dartboards and pool tables, too. **BlackBook**

RoHan Lounge 3809 Geary Blvd. (2nd Ave.) (415) 221-5095 Pity they opened this Asian soju lounge, because we were thinking what this area needed was another Irish bar. First-class chill zone with bamboo walls, velvet couch, and elegantly low lighting in glamour-starved neighborhood. Blended cocktails with names like Confucius and Numbchuck, or straight-up soju for those who mean business.

Trad'r Sam 6150 Geary Blvd. (25th Ave.) (415) 221-0773 Seedy Richmond gathering place for recent college grads still into hard-drinking, hard-flirting pickup scene. Polynesian drink specials are only differentiating factor. Sugar + coconut + alcohol = some hurtin' ahead.

Yancy's Saloon 734 Irving St. (9th Ave.) (415) 665-6551 Sports on the big screen, darts in the back corner, couches. No real character to this place, but young professionals and UCSF students gather here for lack of better neighborhood alternatives.

_____

_____

_____

_____

_____

_____

_____

_____

_____

_____

_____

_____

_____

_____

_____

_____

_____

_____

"But oh, San Francisco! It is and has everything... you wouldn't think that such a place as

San Francisco could exist. The lobsters, clams, crabs. Oh, Cat, what food for you.

And all the people are open and friendly." —Dylan Thomas

BERKELEY & OAKLAND (map p. 136-141)

Hell, we're suckers for an underdog, so we've got our money on the East Bay. It's kinda like a Brooklyn thing: **For those who make the trek across the water, true discovery awaits.** Berkeley's got the university and the heavy '60s cred, but Oakland's the one poised for a comeback, like the scrappy fighter who's been down and out a few too many times. When SF seems too posh and we're digging something grittier, we know where to go. We'll start with the underground loft parties in West Oakland and Al Green onstage at the mind-blowing Paramount Theatre. The downtown district is still hit or miss, with a few cool dives near **Jack London Square** and some dodgy shit going on after dark. **Rockridge** and **Piedmont** you've known about for a while, as in the truffle dinners at **Oliveto** and the hype for new classics like **Dopo**. Keep your eye on the up-and-coming Temescal strip. As for **Berkeley**, where hippie clichés are alive and well, think tie-dye and headscarves, health food and juice bars, heated opinion and hearts on sleeves. Baby punks keep the flame alive outside **Gilman Street Project**, while honky-tonk hos at the **Acme Bar** down dollar shots of Jim Beam at midnight. Hit the so-called gourmet ghetto to order politics on a plate. And what else is there to say about **Chez Panisse**, the ultimate Cali foodie destination? What other restaurant would give a farmer a standing ovation? Find us putting back the cider flight at **Cesar's**, rollin' in the dough at **Pizzaiolo**, bowing down to the great McCoy Tyner at **Yoshi's**, and grooving till close at the **Shattuck Down Low**.

RESTAURANTS Berkeley & Oakland

À Côté 5478 College Ave. (Lawton & Taft Aves.) (510) 655-6469 French. The Emerald City had a bar? Dark green scene and place to be seen. You can argue about the décor, but why bother when you can look good, eat well, and play Dorothy does Dallas with a Grappa Strega in one hand and a Pappy Van Winkle's in the other. Click your heels and order mussels with Pernod from the wood oven with a heaping plate of pommes frites. $30

Ajanta 1888 Solano Ave. (Alameda) (510) 526-4373 Indian. Regional dishes in elegant space. Quality aesthetic, nicely lit. Go when the fog rolls in and you crave cultural transport. Get the vegetable pakora and anything that simmers in curry. Fabulous and fresh. Don't forget extra chutney. You'll never go back to all-you-can-eat buffets again. $22

Bay Wolf 3853 Piedmont Ave. (Montell St. & Rio Vista Ave.) (510) 655-6004 American. Beauty and time making peace in converted Victorian. Pretty wine list, naughty where it ought to be, much like the food. Try duck liver flan with pickled onions and grilled bread, then bouillabaisse. Relaxed sophisticates, ladies lunching, impromptu dinner treat. You oughta linger. $40

Cha-Ya 1686 Shattuck Ave. (Virginia St.) (510) 981-1213 Vegetarian Japanese. Don't let veggie/vegan thing scare you. Just let your inner hippie shine on because this place is good (for you), cheap, and worth the wait for one of 25 coveted seats. Tempura sushi, agedashi tofu, summer green roll, yoga instructors, morbidly enlightened film students, sake and sea vegetable—all a must. Stick around till closing time to see cooks scarfing down fried eggs and hot dogs. $15

The Cheese Board Collective 1512 Shattuck Ave. (Cedar & Vine Sts.) (510) 549-3055 Bakery/Cheese Shop/Takeout Pizza. Down-with-the boss-man, worker-owned biz in gourmet ghetto that sells the best brioche, pecan roll, and loaf of sourdough beer rye this side of capitalism. Beware mob scene at cheese counter. Plan a baguette party and head to the park, or line up for pizza next door where Berkeley High jazz students play till the dough runs out. $10

Chez Panisse Café and Restaurant 1517 Shattuck Ave. (Cedar St.) (510) 548-5049/-5525 French. Cook Werner Herzog's shoe circa 1980, drink some Bandol, break bread with Berkeley radicals, drink some more Bandol, build organic empire and they will come. Thirty-four years of seminal eats that fed the revolution. What more can be said of Alice Waters and her everlasting gobstopper of perfection? Politics you can eat with a fork. +$45
BlackBook

Dona Tomas 5004 Telegraph Ave. (49th & 51st Sts.) (510) 450-0522 Mexican. Little jewel in Oakland's Temescal, like the white gardenia in Frida's raven locks. Fancified Mexican dinners and tequila samplers without murals. Always packed because locals are suave, staff is cool, and organic chicken enchiladas with Oaxacan black mole are worth the $17 price tag. Outdoor patio and dimly lit bar make this a double-up-on-the-margarita, stay-another-momentita kind of place. $31

Dopo 4293 Piedmont Ave. (Echo Ave.) (510) 652-3676 Italian/Pizza. Two boys from Oliveto dishing up amazing Italian to cool and friendly, anything-goes crowd. Tiny and cute, like the menu. Eat at one of two outside tables. Some nights it's worth tasting everything. Carpaccio, tortelloni, pizza dopo, bottle of chianti. Tight service. East Bay Superga. +$35

Eccolo 1820 Fourth St. (Hearst & Virginia Sts.) (510) 644-0444 Italian. Big, open, cool tones of yellow and blue. Not a speck of art on the walls, Milano moderno style. Newly opened, but already a scene. Chez Panisse alum Christopher Lee took his show across town to plate up Dow Jones millennium meal that's worth every bite. Grazie mille. $40

El Huarache Azteca 3842 International Blvd. (38th & 39th Aves.) (510) 533-2395 Mexican. Hola ese, no super burritos or spinach tortilla wraps here! But bringing your hooptie way out to this Oakland barrio is worth it. Get the enchiladas de mole or huarache with cactus and carne asada. Living la vida hangover? Sunday's pot of pozole is the cure-all. $15

Everett & Jones BBQ 1955 San Pablo Ave. (University & Hearst Aves.) (510) 548-8261 Barbecue. Dude, when the surf's blown out, head back early and stop here for an awesome plate of hot-ass pork ribs. Smoke a bowl to make room for more bitchin'-in-your-belly goodness. Local chain known as the best. Order your sliced beef brisket spicy and wonder if the smell of charcoal-smokin' flesh is your own. $10

Gregoire 2109 Cedar St. (Walnut St. & Shattuck Ave.) (510) 883-1893 French. Teeny-tiny with big dollop of contagious, come-'n'-get-it-while-it's-hot, neighborhood joie de vivre. Friendly regulars know to get crispy potato puffs and tomato braised chicken sandwich with cheese. Only three counter seats and two outside tables, so plan on takeout. Seasonal, local, organic spiel. $20

Lois The Pie Queen 851 60th St. (Adeline St.) (510) 658-5616 Soul Food. Best greasy-spoon, breakfast-n-grits, family-lovin', pork-chops-and-buttermilk-drinkin', heal-a-meal you and Reggie Jackson ever had. Breakfast, lunch and dinner, Oakland historical landmark—your new favorite Sunday joint. It's not a Twin Peaks slice of pie, but the lemon ice box is pretty darn satisfying. -$15

O Chamé 1830 4th St. (Virginia St. & Hearst Ave.) (510) 841-8783 Japanese. Palettes in search of afterglow find respite from upscale shopping on trendy 4th Street. Take a date, sip champagne oolong, slurp soba with smoked trout, feel beautiful. Order tuna sashimi with horseradish sauce, vinegared cucumbers with shiso leaf, and caramel balsamic gelato to qualify for multiple orgasms. Mmmm. +$30

Oliveto Café and Restaurant 5655 College Ave. (Shafter Ave.) (510) 547-5356 Italian. Paul Bertolli's masterpiece of Renaissance bourgeois. Elegant huntsman's supper room. Indulgence spilleth over, and so does the Barolo. House made salami, delicate pasta, rotisserie meats. Would be heaven if it weren't so subdued, wrinkly, and overrun with the subtle snob. Sunday brunch when the in-laws come to town. +$45

Pearl Oyster Bar & Restaurant 5634 College Ave. (Shafter & Ocean View Aves.) (510) 654-5426 Seafood. Current like the sea. Out with the old, in with the new, metallic and blue. Another cool nip and tuck in Rockridge facelift. Slam back a few Hama Hamas, some local Hog Islands, and a martini glass of spicy raw tuna poke while old Brando plays behind the bar. Where James Bond would go to meet the mermaid of his dreams. $35

Pizzaiolo 5008 Telegraph Ave. (51st St.) (510) 652-4888 Pizza/Italian. Heads up, East Bay insiders: Temescal's officially on the map. Yet another Chez Panisse grad worships at altar of local, organic, sustainable gods. Heard it all before, but hey, no one's complaining. Perfect thin-crust pies sailing out of wood-fired oven, brilliantly simple polenta and broccoli rabe reimagined. Long wait and no reservations, just 'cuz they can. Neighborhood joint deluxe. $30 ☆ **BlackBook**

Pyung Chang Restaurante 4701 Telegraph Ave. (47th St.) (510) 658-9040 Korean. Why do the cleanse when there's kim chee? One of many side dishes that drop to your table, but order it in a cauldron-hot tofu stew. Get green onion pancakes and bulgogi with sautéed onions. Romantic in that spicy-fermented kind of way. Clears your gut and hopefully your mind. Chef's day-off favorite. $18

The Smokehouse 3115 Telegraph Ave. (Woolsey & Prince Sts.) (510) 845-3640 Hamburgers. So few places are open late in Berkeley, you gotta take advantage. Old-school, blue-collar lunch scene, flippin' patties since 1951. Get it while it's hot and your digestion cooperates. Late-night burgers till 1 a.m., chili cheese fries, malted shakes that'll make you want to strap on the roller skates and show off your buns Heather Graham–style. OK, don't. Please? Really. $7

Thai Buddhist Temple Mongkolratanaram 1911 Russell St. (Otis St. & Martin Luther King Jr. Way) (510) 849-3419 Southeast Asian. Sunday brunch only. Cash in American currency for plastic tokens at outdoor, around-the-world-in-one-day, Thai extravaganza without jet lag or parasites. Sticky rice is steaming, incense is burning, curries are brewing, noodles are frying, grease is flying. Bring friends. Foreign-country chaos the good old-fashioned way. Fill your plate and go back for more—as a tourist, you're required to overdo it. +$10

Vik's Chaat Corner 726 Allston Way (4th & 5th Sts.) (510) 644-4412 Indian. Loud sitar music, saris, and random lunch crowd meets Indian-style small plates that are cheap like crack but way better. Newly expanded garage/warehouse, zero looks but a lotta funk, best-kept used-to-be-a-secret that everyone loves. Order at the counter and take a seat. Puff puri, alutiki chola, any daily special. Take a Bollywood set break—only open for lunch. -$10

NIGHTLIFE Berkeley & Oakland

Acme Bar 2115 San Pablo Ave. (Addison St.) (510) 644-2226 Wanted: black-leather-jacket-wearing, occasional coke-snorting folk looking to have fun, play some old punk on the jukebox, and have a place to call their own. Fringe scene and friendly-neighbor hangout. Honky Tonk Mondays, Punk Rock Wednesdays. Trashy Thursdays all week long.

Albatross Pub 1822 San Pablo Ave. (Hearst Ave. & Delaware St.) (510) 843-2473 Oldest pub in Berkeley. Glimmerin' moon-shine, Coleridge style. The Bird, man. Chill out, have a great beer on tap in a sexy glass, play darts, listen to music, play a board game (Balderdash, Boggle, Connect Four?), bring your dog—it's that kind of place. Like your grandpa's old hang, in the coolest of ways.

The Alley 3325 Grand Ave. (Santa Clara & Elwood Aves.) (510) 444-8505 Diva of dives where piano karaoke reigns. Man on the keys playing everything from Cole Porter to Patsy Cline, while you and your friends heed the ancient laws of crooning. Old swingers and nerdsome hipsters gather over $8 steaks and a fill-'er-up state of mind. Cash only.

Café Van Kleef 1621 Telegraph Ave. (16th St.) (510) 763-7711 Oaksterdam cool spot put out casting call for flaunters and haunters, so they came. Guys in fedoras, live music, and resident ghost clinking glasses amid chaos of collectibles that line walls, hang from ceiling, and pile up around bar. Ornate with trinkets, but not always so stocked with the booze.

César 1515 Shattuck Ave. (Cedar & Vine Sts.) (510) 883-0222 Sublime. The supreme bar, really. Hip, elegant, down to earth. Penelope Cruz in America. Amazing tapas, endless stock of sherries, perfect French daiquiri. Huge doors that open onto sidewalk, or is that the Spanish seaside? Mojito with a view. Get drunk on life's little arias. ☆

George and Walt's 5445 College Ave. (Kales Ave.) (510) 653-7441 Repeat after me: This is a sports bar. This bar has drinks and sports. The bartender will call you honey. There are pennants and pool tables. Pinball, too. TVs in every corner. Go Raiders!

Jupiter 2181 Shattuck Ave. (Allston Way) (510) 843-8277 Gothic lights and old church pews for sinnin' and grinnin'. Huge back patio for summertime in the city. John Martin of Triple Rock Brewery made this the place for local beers, Mingus Amungus fans, and college dorks. Dependable.

Kingfish Pub 5227 Claremont Ave. (Telegraph Ave.) (510) 655-7373 Who ordered the takeout pizza? Y-chromosomes in favorite pair of sweats connect over brews and a poker table. Lobster shack/baseball dugout where the boys are, and the women…well, there's only one of them. But that just makes her more of a badass.

Kingman's Lucky Lounge 3332 Grand Ave. (Elwood & Santa Clara Aves.) (510) 465-5464 A shot of the superior gene pool, straight up or on the rocks. Plush puppies and drunks-with-standards willing to wait in line to make their move on the dance floor. Fresh. Signature drinks. Get the crushed velvet.

The 924 Gilman Street Project 924 Gilman St. (7th & 8th Sts.) (510) 525-9926 Weekends only. Punk kids line up for all-ages shows. No booze, but rebellion like this don't come in a bottle. Respect for these youngsters, you must have. Nonprofit, nonviolent, underground scene. "At least we know where they are, dear…they could be down some dark alley in the back of a car."

Radio Bar 435 13th St. (Broadway & Franklin Sts.) (510) 451-2889 Sexy like George Michael doing Asian-fetish thing. Just say yes if bartender offers you a Washington apple. Long narrow bar with rotating DJs, breakbeats, underground lounge, and Sunday special black-sweatshirt night. Turns into a party around 1 a.m.

Ruby Room 132 14th St. (Oak & Madison Sts.) (510) 444-7444 Dark, dank, and swank. Old Tahoe tavern scene. Quintessential East Bay scenesters loving tiny dance floor and fourth G&T. Go on Wednesdays for DJ Kitty's soul revue. Pretty babies grooving your ruby glow.

Shattuck Down Low 2284 Shattuck Ave. (Dwight Way & University Ave.) (510) 548-1159 Hidden below the Pasand restaurant, it goes something like this: samba, funk, salsa, hip-hop, reggae, karaoke. Candles, curtains, and booths. However you like it in the underworld, nothing is too low down.

The Starry Plough 3101 Shattuck Ave. (Prince & Woolsey Sts.) (510) 841-2082 Bring your boyfriend, girlfriend, leprechaun—anybody is and always was welcome. Bring your poetry, fiddle, dancing boots, and yer love of the ol'pint to this magical mix-up that's way better than a box of lucky charms. Berkeley hall of famer. Extended happy hour daily from 11 till 7.

Yoshi's 510 Embarcadero West (Clay & Washington Sts.) (510) 238-9200 Live jazz, sushi, supper club. Great date spot with night-on-the-town feel. Mediocre Japanese fare well worth it to reserve a seat. McCoy Tyner, Shirley Horn, oh, it is tight, baby. Good judgment always gives way to musical transcendence. **BlackBook**

_____

_____

_____

_____

_____

_____

_____

_____

_____

_____

_____

_____

_____

_____

"Los Angeles? That's just a big parking lot where you buy a hamburger for the trip

to San Francisco." —John Lennon and Yoko Ono

SAN FRANCISCO HOTELS

It's not about where you're staying, it's about who you wanna be. In a Victorian-corset kinda mood? Dig the cupolas at the **Stanyan Park Hotel**. More on the masters of the universe tip? The world sure seems like your oyster from your tub at the **Four Seasons.** (The Bulgari bubble bath doesn't hurt, either.) Planning a weekend bender with friends? Slap on that "Do Not Disturb" sign at the **Phoenix** and chill by the pool later when you're spun for fun. Paging Sam Spade at the **Pickwick**, Ginsberg and Kerouac at the **Bohème**, bootylicious tube-topped hussy at the **Clift**, and blushing young bride at the **Archbishop's Mansion**. We'll play along. Meet us at the buffet on the **Ritz-Carlton** club level before sealing the deal at the Huntington bar.

Archbishop's Mansion 1000 Fulton St. (Steiner St.) (415) 563-7872 Dove-gray French chateau across Alamo Square Park, next to famous Painted Ladies. Romantic retreat for many a honeymoon. Scarlett O'Hara staircase, rooms with fire-places and let's-get-it-on names like Don Giovanni. Canopied beds and tasseled pillows form strange contrast to hipster record stores and boutiques of Lower Haight just a few blocks away. $145–$495

Clift Hotel 495 Geary St. (Taylor St.) (415) 775-4700 Makes us nostalgic for Ian Schrager's glory days, when the Royalton and Delano were the apex of cool. Now slightly dated in an endearing kind of way, but don't tell the business travelers and sales reps. Rooms full of more retro throwbacks in the form of billowing white drapes, white couches, and mirrored glass dining tables. It's VH1's I Love The '80s! Pretty, doe-eyed staff achingly eager to please. $225–$2,000

Four Seasons Hotel 757 Market St. (4th St.) (415) 633-3000 Traveling NBA teams, old-money politicos, well-kept Hong Kong matrons. Everyone from Bill Clinton to Beck has slumbered here. Tastefully modern halls of muted beige and blue tones, exotic African woods. Hushed, intimate feel of fifth-floor lobby offers womblike retreat from the clatter of Market Street. Thirtysomething hardbody pick-up scene at in-house Sports Club/LA. $320–$4,900

Hotel Adagio 550 Geary St. (Taylor St.) (415) 775-5000 Ornate Spanish Colonial Revival built at dawn of the Depression. Chic, newly renovated interior with over-sized lampshades clustered above marble-topped coffee tables, stark branch arrangements, warm cream and terracotta tones punctuated with abstract paint-ings. Lobby bleeds into atmospheric Cortez restaurant. Handsome, subdued rooms provide tasteful respite. Good deal for the price. $130–$795

Hotel Bijou 111 Mason St. (Eddy St.) (415) 771-1200 Film buff's paradise. Deep moody purples, rich reds, and Op Art zigzag carpeting take you to set of Lost Highway. Heavy velvet curtains enclose Petit Bijou Theatre, which hosts two nightly screenings of SF cinematic gems. Rooms named after locally filmed blockbusters (Cujo to Dirty Harry), embellished with photos of Bay Area movie palaces and geometrically patterned bedspreads in screaming colors. $90–$170

Hotel Bohème 444 Columbus Ave. (Vallejo St.) (415) 433-9111 Street clatter and cafe chatter characterize neighborhood best known for bringing notes from the underground to the surface. Black door with modest awning amid pastry shops and sidewalk tables. Pension-style establishment laden with vintage photos of notorious beatniks and jazz heavyweights. Pick up a copy of Howl from Ferlinghetti's City Lights down the block, and read aloud in room 204. Trust us. $150–$195

Hotel Diva 440 Geary St. (Mason St.) (415) 885-0200 In heart of Theater District, cool green cut-glass entrance leads into trendy modern slicklandia. Multiple TV monitors, backlit cut-agate reception desk, halogen track lights, bird-of-paradise arrangements in silver vases. Donald Judd meets Pokémon. Rooms exude tricked-out Danish appeal, even with weird steel headboards and electric-blue carpet. Staff can be divas, but you should've known that. $115–$575

Hotel Drisco 2901 Pacific Ave. (Broderick St.) (415) 346-2880 Mad dogs, Englishmen, Ashley Judd, and notable variety of upper-crusts make Drisco their home-away-from-mansion. Right in heart of Pacific Heights (a.k.a. Millionaire's Row), atop breezy hill with panoramic views and adorned with windowboxes popping with blooms. Understated elegance, swaddles weary travelers in luxury. In true Hotel California fashion, one guest has stayed five years. $195–$600

Hotel Palomar 12 4th St. (Market St.) (415) 348-1111 Grandiose Victorian-era pistachio-green brick building with classic white granite flourishes. Lobby goes all Asian on us, with sleek parquet floors, shoji screen walls and simple, modern objets d'art. Wall-to-wall leopard carpeting in rooms, Jacuzzi in suites. Fifth Floor restaurant makes all those truffled scallop fantasies come true. $290–$1,000

Hotel Rex 562 Sutter St. (Mason St.) (415) 433-4434 Based on literary salons of mid-20th century and modeled after New York's Algonquin. Corinthian columns, heavily beamed ceilings, dark wainscoting, warm yellow walls painted with Matisse-inspired line drawings, stacks of leather-bound classics inviting intellectual discussion and witty repartee à la Dorothy Parker. Original period artwork and quotes from John Steinbeck to Dashiell Hammett on walls. $155–$340

HOTELS

Hotel Triton 342 Grant Ave. (Bush St.) (415) 394-0500 Hip, lively musician favorite at gaping maw of Chinatown Gate. Lost City of Atlantis appeal, as in jewel-toned lobby sprinkled with fuzzy bubblegum-pink pillows. Celebrity-named bedrooms personally designed by stars themselves (Jerry Garcia, Carlos Santana, Andy Dick?!). Our pick: the Woody Harrelson for its blown-up redwood forest scene and inscriptions of Woody's green-friendly brand of eco-politics. $150–$330

Hotel Vitale 8 Mission St. (Embarcadero) (415) 278-3700 SF's first luxury organic hotel—but think artisanal cheese, not alfalfa sprouts. Ugly exterior (bane of the neighborhood) countered with soothing inoffensive modern furnishings, dreamy bedding, sick views of the Embarcadero (be sure to hit the roof decks). Zen vibe marred by loud and boozy happy hour when Financial District shirts swarm the restaurant patio, but mellows out by early evening. Spirituality deluxe. $199–$1,200 ★

The Huntington Hotel & Nob Hill Spa 1075 California St. (Taylor St.) (415) 474-5400 Built at dawn of Roaring '20s as luxury apartments by Central Pacific Line railroad barons, still oozes posh sophistication. Larger-than-average rooms hung with damask and silk. Big 4 restaurant so old-school it's cool. Star of the show is adjoining Nob Hill Spa, where curving staircase leads to infinity pool dappled with 24-karat gold. Sun-drenched balcony with expansive views. $295–$1,130

Inn San Francisco 943 South Van Ness Ave. (20th St.) (415) 641-0188 Beautifully preserved 1872 Italianate Victorian mansion, once a farm breeding champion racehorses and now the oldest existing hotel in town. Candlelit drawing rooms with fresh flowers, Jacuzzi in latticed gazebo bursting with jasmine and ferns, feather beds, chocolate truffles on pillow, homemade breads and fresh-squeezed OJ at breakfast. It's the good life, baby. All this in the heart of the Mission. $95–$265

The Laurel Inn 444 Presidio Ave. (California St.) (415) 567-8467 Classic early-'60s motor lodge cloaked in modernist comfort. Spacious studio-size rooms lit with sparse, modern lamps, broad beds doused in Southwestern palette. Visiting medical professionals, university types, and members of George Lucas' production team are regulars. Parking is free, pets are welcome, and G Bar's one of the only bars around. Have a paintball fight among eucalyptus groves of nearby Presidio. $165–$195

The Mosser 54 Fourth St. (Mission St.) (415) 986-4400 Can't afford the W or Clift, but would much rather go the IKEA route than suffer quilted floral spreads? The Mosser is the answer. Kickass downtown location, tiny rooms with platform beds and Milano 2000 sensibility plus plenty of the requisite pine. Rent the full-on recording studio if you're a stoned rocker who just wants to stumble to "work" and then stagger back to bed. Super-duper cheap-ass econo rooms for those who'll do the toilet down the hall, sans junkies. $59–$249 ★

Nob Hill Inn 1000 Pine St. (Taylor St.) (415) 673-6080 Quaint and cheery, with wicker love seats, Chippendale chairs, claw-foot tubs, and perennial crystal decanter of sherry at tea time. Lobby cleaved by authentic Edwardian glass elevator imported from London mansion. Once the office of SF's premier madam, now has another sinister secret up its sleeve—its very own Moaning Myrtle. Bring your ghostbuster gun to ghosts-and-vampires tour on Fridays. $125–$275

The Orchard Hotel 665 Bush St. (Powell St.) (415) 362-8878 Diminutive, no-nonsense lobby sports feng shui flow, courtesy of trickling wall fountain and curvilinear bamboo shoots. Entirely nonsmoking facility built at peak of dot-com bubble for largely business clientele. Neatly appointed rooms with DVD and free DSL, harlequin drapes hung over double-paned windows to cloister overworked execs. $150–$370

The Parker Guest House 520 Church St. (17th St.) (415) 621-3222 Mostly gay guesthouse at edge of Castro, one block from Dolores Park. Dark wood paneling and deep green walls in foyer, creamy parlor with grand piano and cozy fireplace. Airy breakfast nook overlooking sylvan garden with rosebushes and fountain. Steam room tucked amid the hydrangeas. Mind you don't trip over Parker (the inn's namesake) and Porter, cuddly pugs who reign supreme. $120–$200

Phoenix Hotel 601 Eddy St. (Larkin St.) (415) 776-1380 Strictly rock 'n' roll hotel plunked down in infamous Tenderloin. Not (we repeat, not) for those looking for quiet getaway. Mod '50s no-fuss tropical bungalows (think Auntie Mame in the Bahamas). Balconies overlook pool lit like Ziggy Stardust concert, and you never know when you'll be woken up by Dogstar or the Chili Peppers partying in its clear blue waters. $110–$260

The Pickwick Hotel 85 5th St. (Mission St.) (415) 421-7500 Faded '40s charm like Hollywood version of Dickens. Popular with starlets back in the day. Scene from The Maltese Falcon (Bogart shoots the Fat Man) filmed in one of the eighth-floor rooms. It's said Capone stashed a fortune here—but when the safe was cracked, there was nothing but dust. Quaint and cozy, without hint of a sinister past. Kitty-corner to San Francisco Chronicle headquarters, where more current intrigues are uncovered. $119–$169

The Ritz-Carlton San Francisco 600 Stockton St. (California St.) (415) 296-7465 What more needs to be said? Monolithic pillared 1909 structure slightly resembling the White House. Culinary superstar Ron Siegel (only American to defeat an Iron Chef!) at helm of kitchen. Marble bathrooms, Frette linens, lots of other swish stuff. Our secret: Stay on Club Level, and stuff yourself silly with five ridiculously overflowing spreads of free food and drink daily. $365–$4,800

Sir Francis Drake Hotel 450 Powell St. (Sutter St.) (415) 392-7755 Lavish European rococo swathed in rich royal colors in lobby of 1928 gem. Just one block up from Union Square on cable-car line. "See no evil, hear no evil, speak no evil" Beefeaters in traditional palace garb provide perfect beginning to evening of naughty decadence, as you sneak up to 21st floor for jazzy nightcap at Harry Denton's Starlight Lounge. $140–$700

Stanyan Park Hotel 750 Stanyan St. (Waller St.) (415) 751-1000 Bordering Golden Gate Park, built by slick saloon owner in 1905 in spurt of Queen Anne meets Beaux-Arts Classicism. Airy rooms in pink and sage that cosset cultivated clientele. Cupola rooms with four-poster beds, suites with parlors and kitchenettes. Hike through the fields where bison roam, or don a kimono and visit the Japanese Tea Garden (for which fortune cookies were invented). $130–$315

24 Henry Guesthouse 24 Henry St. (Noe & Sanchez Sts.) (415) 864-5686 Your own version of Tales of the City. Step into an ultra-homey parlor of funky, mismatched vintage furniture, from Victorian curio-cabinets to pared-down Bauhaus buffets. Serene residential setting bursting with flora, just a stone's throw from the Castro. You never know who'll show up to breakfast in his wife's clothing, or when a queen to rival RuPaul will step out of a cab. $55–$130

W Hotel 181 3rd St. (Howard St.) (415) 777-5300 Fanciful frolicking fun! Sleekly appointed hotel has co-opted the concept of yuppie Wonderland. Three-story octagonal glass entrance leads straight to the bar. Overstuffed leather and velvet chairs, bowls of green apples, Dr. Seuss–inspired floral arrangements. Dark hallways and tiny rooms drive guests straight back down to lobby. New Bliss spa to soak weary feet in. $200–$2,000

The Westin St. Francis 335 Powell St. (Geary St.) (415) 397-7000 Spectacular view that makes you feel like you own the city. Staff that makes you feel like you own them. This place is so money, they've literally been laundering it (via a state-of-the-art silver-cleaning system) since 1938. Heavily coiffed blue-haired ladies dripping with gems, pug under one arm and Pekinese under the other. Armani suits and high rollers in the lobby. Star chef Michael Mina in the house. Twinsets required. $180–$2,900

_____

_____

_____

_____

_____

_____

_____

_____

_____

_____

_____

_____

_____

"This is the friendliest city in the world." —Joe DiMaggio

_____

Jefferson St
Beach St
Pier 33
Pier 31
Pier 29
Powell St
Stockton St
Grant Ave
Kearny St
Pfieffer St
Chestnut St
Pier 27
Winthrop St
Lombard St
Child St
Greenwich St
Pier 23
Jasper Pl
Filbert St
Pier 19
Roach
Alta St
Pier 17
Macondray Ln
Washington Square Park
Union St
Pier 15
Columbus Ave
Castle St
Commerce St
Pier 9
Leavenworth St
Vallejo St
Pier 7
Jones St
Taylor St
Mason St
Powell St
Stockton St
Montgomery St
Kearny St
Sansome St
Broadway
Pier 3
Pier 1
John St
Gold St
Battery St
Custom House Pl
Jackson St
San Francisco B
Priest St
Stone St
Ross Aly
Beckett St
Collier
Merchant St
Washington St
Pier 2
Pleasant St
Clay St
Waverly Pl
Commercial St
Leidesdorff St
Sacramento St
Davis St
Cushman St
Spring St
Clay St
Halleck St
Drumm St
California St
Wetmore St
Juice St
Quincy St
Pine St
Front St
Bush St
Belden Pl
Trinity Pl
Claude Ln
Mission St
Main St
Spear St
The Embarcadero
Cosmo Pl
Campton Pl
Robert Kirk Ln
Ecker
Shaw Al
Fremont St
1st St
Beale St
Folsom St
Shannon St
Maiden Ln
New Montgomery St
2nd St
Ecker St
Essex St
Elwood St
Cyril Magnin St
Stevenson St
Pier
Cohen Pl
Jessie St
Howard St
Bayside Village Pl
SAN FRANCISCO – OAKLAND BAY BRIDGE
Pie
Golden Gate Ave
Minna St
Bonifacio St
Rizal St
Harrison St
Bryant St
Federal St
Delancey St
Pier
Market St
Natoma St
Galleria Ln
Stillman St
Taber Pl
Variney Pl
Brannan St
Pier
Stevenson St
5th St
6th St
Minna St
Natoma St
Tehama St
Clementina St
Falmouth
Shipley St
Clara St
Welsh St
Freelon St
Ritch St
3rd St
2nd St
Stanford St
Gale St
Julia St
9th St
8th St
7th St
Russ St
Sherman St
Harriet St
Moss St
Bluxome St
Townsend St
King St
Berry St
Langton St
Ahern Way
Clyde St
Clara St
Morris St
4th St
5th St
Pier 46B
Ransom St
Harrison St
80

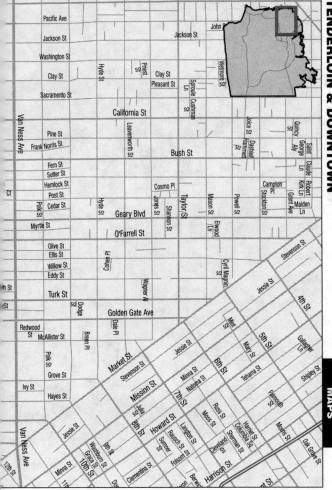

Pier 35

Pier 33

Pier 31

Pier 29

San Francisco Bay

Pier 27

Grant Ave

Vandewater St

Midway St

Water St

Pfeiffer St

Francisco St

Chestnut St

Fielding St

Chestnut St

Winthrop St

Pier 23

Lombard St

Jansen St

Chiloc St

Telegraph Hill Blvd

Greenwich St

Pier 19

Valparaiso St

Filbert St

Filbert St

Alta St

Pier 17

Washington Square Park

Jasper St

Varennes St

Genoa Pl

Sonoma St

Castle St

Union St

Pier 15

Bannam

Grant Ave

Commerce St

Green St

Pier 9

Taylor St

Mason St

Churchill St

Powell St

Stockton St

Fresno St

Romolo Pl

Kearny St

Montgomery St

Sansome St

Vallejo St

Davis St

Broadway

Front St

The Embarcadero

Salmon St

Wayne Pl

John St

Jackson St

Columbus Ave

Osgood Pl

Gold St

Pacific Ave

Jackson St

Pier

Trenton St

Stone St

Beckett St

Went-worth Pl

Ross Aly

Spofford St

Lum Aly

Water U

Merchant St

Hotaling

Custom House Pl

Washington St

Merchant St

Drumm St

Wetmore St

Collier St

Waverly Pl

Papoda

Commercial St

Clay St

Sproule Ln

Cushman St

Spring St

Leidesdorff St

Halleck St

Sacramento St

Davis St

California St

Joice St

Stockton St

Quincy St

George Aly

Belden Pl

Pine St

Front St

Market St

Spear St

Mason St

Dashiell Hammett St

Saint George Aly

Claude Ln

Bush St

Tilman Pl

Mission St

Main St

Spear St

Powell St

Campton Pl

Kirk Ln

Robert

Kearny St

Maiden Ln

Lick Pl

Stevenson St

Ecker St

Jessie St

1St St

Beale St

Howard St

Fremont St

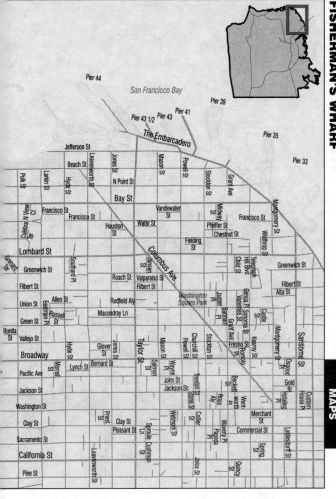

FISHERMAN'S WHARF

San Francisco Bay

Pier 44
Pier 43 1/2
Pier 43
Pier 41
Pier 39
Pier 35
Pier 33

The Embarcadero

Jefferson St
Beach St
Bay St
N Point St
Francisco St
Water St
Vandewater St
Houston St
Lombard St
Greenwich St
Filbert St
Union St
Green St
Vallejo St
Broadway
Pacific Ave
Jackson St
Washington St
Clay St
Sacramento St
California St
Pine St

Polk St
Larkin St
Hyde St
Leavenworth St
Jones St
Mason St
Powell St
Stockton St
Grant Ave
Montgomery St

Columbus Ave

Washington Square Park

MAPS

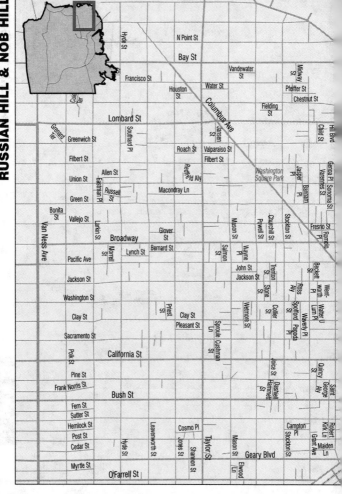

Joice St
Dashiell Hammett St
Bush St
Sutter St
Hyde St
Post St
Leavenworth St
Cosmo Pl
Myrtle St
Geary Blvd
Mason St
Powell St
Stockton St
Campton Pl
Daniel Burnham Ct
Olive St
O'Farrell St
Cohn Magnin St
Willow St
Taylor St
Wagner
Polk St
Turk St
Franklin St
Elm St
Golden Gate Ave
Redwood St
Jessie St
Stevenson St
Minna St
Hunt St
Hawthorne St
Monterey St
2nd St
3rd St
Mary's
Gallagher
Bonifacio St
Lapu Lapu St
Rizal St
Grove St
Market St
Minna St
Natoma St
Clementina St
Falmouth
Shipley St
Clara St
Hayes St
Howard St
Ben St
Washburn St
Tehama St
Russ St
Moss St
Columbia St
Sherman St
Harriet St
Harrison St
Mabini St
Oak Grove St
Morris St
Welsh St
4th St
Hickory St
Lily St
Rose St
Van Ness Ave
12th St
Grace St
Lafayette St
Ringold St
Gordon St
Berwick Pl
Herich Pl
Bryant St
Ahern Way
Boardman Pl
Gilbert St
5th St
Kissling St
Norfolk St
Dore St
Branan St
Townsend St
7th St
6th St
McCoppin St
Elgin Park
Plum St
13th St
Jessie
Erie St
Erie St
14th St
Trainor St
Division St
Alameda St
Berry St
Channel St
King St
Owens St
Woodward St
Stevenson St
Julian Ave
Minna St
Natoma St
Wiese St
Caledonia St
Adair St
15th St
15th St
York St
Shotwell St
Kansas St
San Bruno Ave
Hooper St
Irwin St
Hubbell St
8th St
Wisconsin St
16th St
Valencia St
Lapidge St
Mission St
Clapp St
S Van Ness Ave
Folsom St
Treat Ave
Alabama St
Florida St
Bryant St
York St
Hampshire St
Harrison St
17th St
Utah St
Potrero Ave
Vermont St
Rhode Island St
De Haro St
Carolina St
18th St
Franklin St
Golden Gate Ave

MAPS

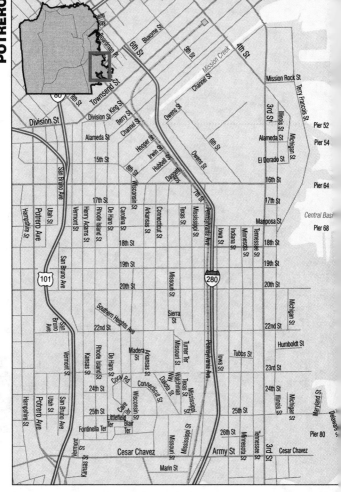

Merchant St
Commercial St
Clay St
Sacramento St
California St
Waverly Pl
Spring St
Halleck St
Pine St
Market St
Quincy St
Belden Pl
Bush St
Montgomery St
Sansome St
Battery St
Campton Pl
Grant Ave
Kearny St
Stockton St
Mission St
Main St
Spear St
Steuart St
The Embarcadero

Pier 24
Pier 26
Pier 28
Pier 30
Pier 32

Beale St
Fremont St
Folsom St
Jessie St
Stevenson St
Annie St
Jane St
New Montgomery St
Minna St
Natoma St
1st St
2nd St
Stevenson St
Ecker Pl
Tehama St
James Lick Fwy
Clementina St
Essex St
Guy Pl
Lansing
Harrison St

Jessie St
4th St
Howard St
Mabini St
Bonifacio St
Rizal St
Lapu Lapu St
Hawthorne St
Hunt St
Sherman St
S Park Av
Tabor Pl
Federal St
Bryant St
Rincon St
Bayside Village Pl

Fremont St

Pier 34
Pier 36
Pier 38
Pier 40

San Francisco Bay

5th St
Mary St
Gallagher
Shipley St
Clara St
Welsh St
Zoe St
Freelon St
Ritch St
Clarence Pl
3rd St
Braman St
Colin P
Kelly Jr St
Stafford Pl
Delancy St
Gate St
Jack London Aly
King St

South Beach Harbor

Tehama St
Clementina St
Falmouth St
Harriet St
Merlin St
Oak Grove St
Morris St
Barry St

Pier 46B
Pier 48C   China Basin

Sherman St
Ahern Way
Boardman Pl
5th St
Bluxome St
4th St
Townsend St

Pier 48

Bryant St
Gilbert St
Brannan St
7th St
6th St
Channel St
Mission Creek
Mission Rock St
4th St
3rd St
Illinois St
Terry Francois St

Pier 50

8th St
Division St
King St
Berry St
Channel St
Owens St
Alameda St
6th St
3rd St
Alameda St
Michigan St
El Dorado St
Pier 52
Pier 54

15th St
8th St
Hooper St
Irwin St
Hubbell St
Owens St

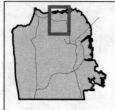

San Francisco Bay

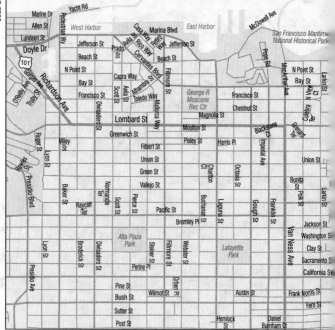

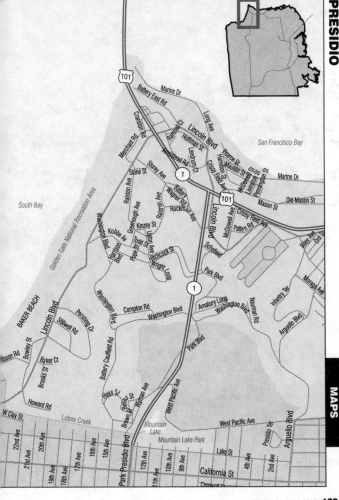

101

Marine Dr

Battery East Rd

Cranston Rd

Merchant Rd

Long Ave

Lincoln Blvd

Hoffman St

Pearce St

Pershing Dr

Lincoln St

Cranston Rd

Ct

San Francisco Bay

1

Storey Ave

Stone St

Ralston Ave

Wagner Rd

Battery

Ralston Ave

Ambrised Rd

Lenorum Ct

Hamlon St

Mcdowell Ave

Cristo Field Ave

Marine Dr

Old Mason St

Kobbe Av

Greenough Ave

Kinzey St

Upton Ave

Washington Blvd

Harrison Blvd

Todd St

Pope St

Hitchcock St

Wright Loop

Ruckman Ave

Lincoln Blvd

McDowell Ave

Patten Rd

Mason St

Crissy Field Ave

South Bay

Golden Gate National Recreation Area

101

Schofield

Park Blvd

Riley Ave

Ord St

Moraga Ave

Pershing Dr

Washington Blvd

Compton Rd

Washington Blvd

Amatury Loop

Washington Blvd

Nauman Rd

Infantry Ter

Arguello Blvd

BAKER BEACH

Lincoln Blvd

Stillwell Rd

Battery Caulfield Rd

Park Blvd

1

Bowley St

Baker Ct

Brooks St

Gibson Rd

Hays St

Brown St

Bliss St

Wyman Ave

West Pacific Ave

Howard Rd

W Clay St

Lobos Creek

Park Presidio Blvd

Mountain Lake

Mountain Lake Park

West Pacific Ave

Presidio Ter

Arguello Blvd

22nd Ave

21st Ave

20th Ave

19th Ave

18th Ave

17th Ave

16th Ave

15th Ave

12th Ave

11th Ave

10th Ave

9th Ave

Lake St

4th Ave

2nd Ave

California St

Cornwall St

101

Marine Dr

Battery East Rd

Long Ave

Lincoln Ave

Cranston Rd

Merchant Rd

Ralston Ave

Hoffman St

Marine Dr

Pearce St

Hamilton St

Crissy Field Rd

Lincoln Blvd

Storey Ave

Battery Wagner Rd

Ralston Ave

McDowell St

Livington St

Pennington St

Marine Dr

Golden Gate National Recreation Area

Mason St

Jaus

Mitchell

Marshall St

1

101

Mason St

Old Mason St

Vallejo St

Greenough Ave

Pipe St

Wright Loop

McDowell St

Crissy Field Ave

Young St

Taylor Rd

Montgomery St

Anza St

Sheridan Ave

Greten St

Mesa Ave

Funston Ave

Lincoln Blvd

Gorgas Ave

Girard Rd

Kenr

Torney

Harrison Blvd

Schofield

Park Blvd

Moraga Ave

Hardie Ave

Anza Ave

Presidio Blvd

Presidio Blvd

1

Compton Rd

Washington Blvd

Amatury Long

Washington Blvd

Nauman Rd

Infantry Ter

Arguello Blvd

Hicks Rd

Barnard St

Fernandez St

McArthur Ave

Sumner St

MacArthur Ave

Morton St

Gary Jordan

JS Faichildi

Rodriquez St

Clark St

Salty Rd

Shafte

Hays St

Brown St

Wyman Ave

Park Blvd

Park Blvd

West Pacific Ave

Quarry Rd

Walken Ct

El Polin Loop

Portola St

West Pacific Ave

Mountain Lake

Mountain Lake Park

West Pacific Ave

Presidio Ter

Arguello Blvd

Washington St

Cherry St

Maple St

Spruce St

Locust St

Laurel St

Lake St

California St

Park Presidio Blvd

Funston Ave

12th Ave

11th Ave

10th Ave

9th Ave

4th Ave

3rd Ave

2nd Ave

Cornwall St

Clement St

5th Ave

Mayfair Dr

Euclid Ave

Jordan Ave

Commonwealth Ave

Parker Ave

Ins Ave

Heather Ave

Spruce

Manzanita Ave

Collins St

Blak

Laurel

Lupin

Palm Ave

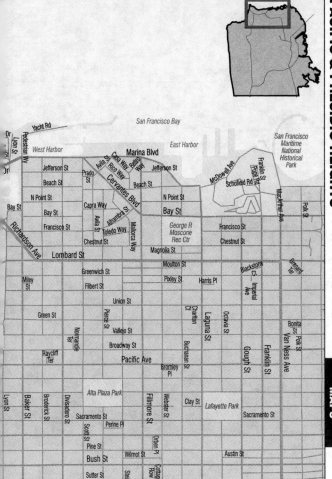

Normandie Ter
Vallejo St
Raycliff Ter
Broadway St
Pacific Ave
Bromley Pl
Buchanan St
Laguna St
Gough St
Franklin St
Van Ness Ave

Alta Plaza Park
Clay St
Lafayette Park
Laurel St
Walnut St
Lyon St
Broderick St
Sacramento St
Perine Pl
Filmore St
Webster St
Gough St
California St
Presidio Ave
Pine St
Baker St
Divisadero St
Bush St
Wilmot St
Open Pl
Cottage Row
Austin St
Sutter St
Avery St
Laurel St
Lupine Ave
Post St
Masonic Ave
Leona Ter
Garden St
Geary Blvd
Hemlock St
Emerson St
Wood St
Sonora Ln
Collins St
Zampa Ln
Galilee Ln
Laguna St
Daniel Burnham Ct
Cleary Ct
O'Farrell St
Barcelona Ave
Terra Vista Ave
Beideman St
Ellis St
Byington St
Hollis St
Inca Ln
Willow St
Eddy St
Jean Way
Ewing Ter
Vega St
Nido Ave
Encanto Ave
Fortuna Ave
Eddie St
Dolger Al
Larch St
Larch St
Anza Vista Ave
Saint Josephs Ave
Seymour St
Turk St
Jefferson Square
Tamalpais Ter
Annapolis Ter
Hemway Ter
Elm St
Golden Gate Ave
Elm St
McAllister St
Redw
Fulton St
Central Ave
Lyon St
Baker St
Broderick St
Alamo Square
Filmore St
Ash St
Birch St
Grove St
Ivy St
Linden St
Octavia St
Franklin St
Ivy
Banneker Way
Hayes St
Fell St
Oak St
Hickory St
Ashbury St
Masonic Ave
Central Ave
Lyon St
Divisadero St
Scott St
Pierce St
Steiner St
Page St
Lily St
Lily St
Rose St
Haight St
Laussat St
Waller St
Waller St
Pearl St
10th St
Brady St
Gough St
Buena Vista Park
Carmelita St
Lloyd St
Potomac St
Hermann St
Duboce Ave
Reservoir St
Rosemont Pl
Stevenson St
Clinton Park
Plum St
13th St
Buena Vista Av
Castro St
Alpine Ter
Divisadero St
Noe St
Sanchez St
Belcher St
Brosnan St
Clinton Park
Otis St
Naomi St
Milma St
Piedmont St
Roosevelt
14th St
Walter St
Landers St
Hidalgo Ter
Woodward St
Julian Ave
Mission St
Caledonia St
Ashbury Ter
Masonic Ave
Museum Way
Henry St
Jessie St
Delmar St
Flint St
15th St
Beaver St
Market St
Alert Aly
Sharon St
Church St
Dolores St
Ord Cy
Saturn St
16th St
Sanchez St

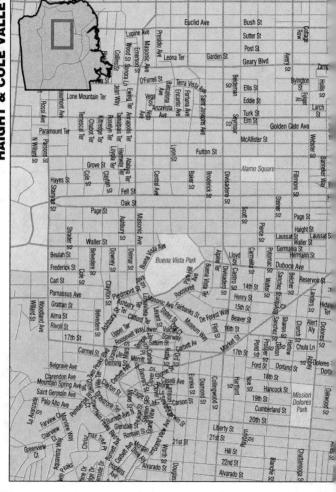

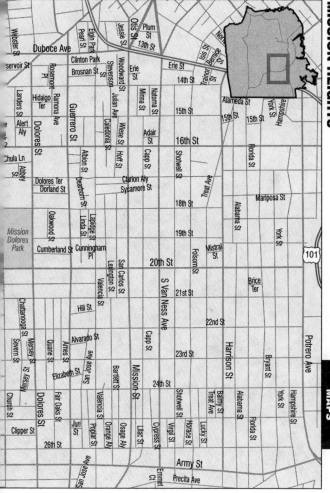

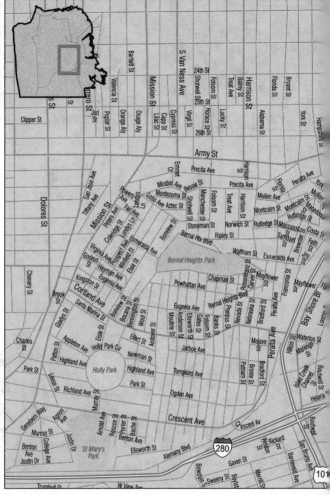

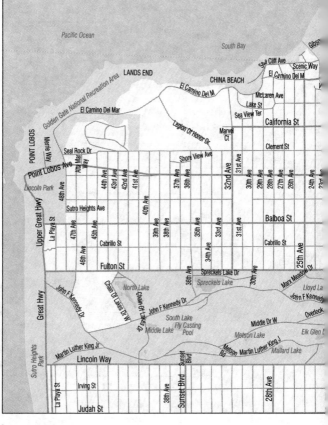

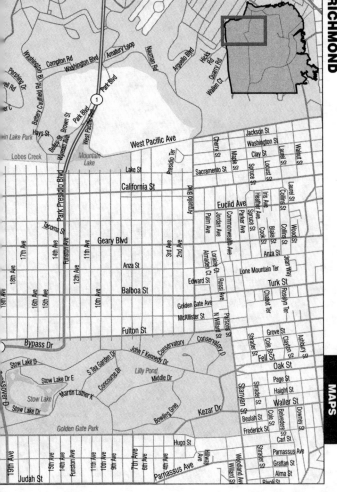

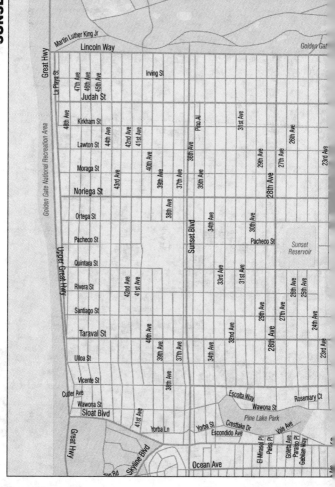

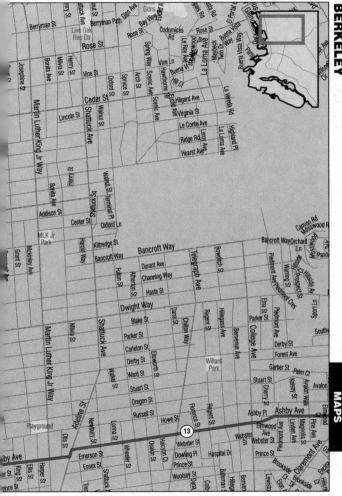

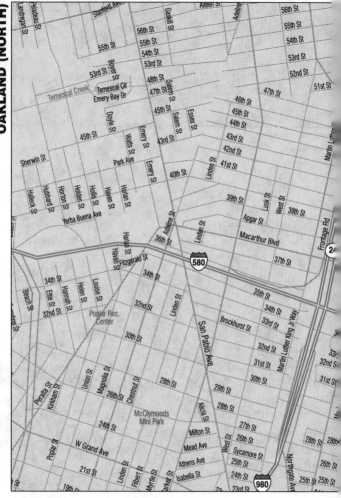

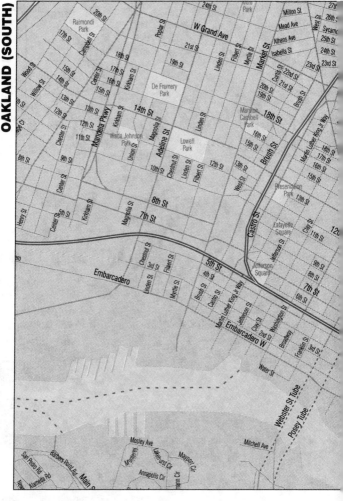

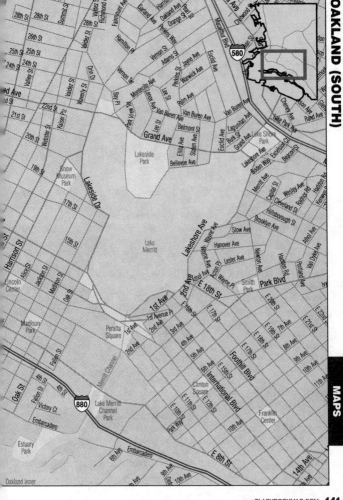

INDEX

INDEX

INDEX